LEVEL 7 Supplemental

EXAM SERIES

By Glory St. Germain ARCT RMT MYCC UMTC &
Shelagh McKibbon-U'Ren RMT UMTC

ULTIMATE
MUSIC THEORY

GSG MUSIC

Enriching Lives Through Music Education

ISBN: 978-1-990358-15-9

The Ultimate Music Theory™ Program

Enriching Lives Through Music Education

The Ultimate Music Theory™ Workbooks & Answer Books Program includes:

UMT Rudiments Workbooks for Prep 1, Prep 2, Basic, Intermediate, Advanced & Complete
UMT Exam Series (Set #1 & Set #2) for Preparatory, Basic, Intermediate & Advanced

Supplemental Workbooks for PREP LEVEL, LEVELS 1 - 8 & COMPLETE LEVEL
UMT Supplemental Exam Series for LEVEL 5, LEVEL 6, LEVEL 7 & LEVEL 8

The Ultimate Music Theory Program is the *Way to Score Success* as UMT helps students prepare for nationally recognized theory examinations including the Royal Conservatory of Music.

Library and Archives Canada Cataloguing in Publication. UMT Workbooks & Exam Series /Glory St. Germain & Shelagh McKibbon-U'Ren. Respect Copyright. All rights reserved. GlorylandPublishing.com

Ultimate Music Theory Rudiments Exam Series

GP - EPS1	ISBN: 978-1-927641-00-2	Preparatory Rudiments Exams Set #1
GP - EPS1A	ISBN: 978-1-927641-08-8	Preparatory Exams Answers Set #1
GP - EPS2	ISBN: 978-1-927641-01-9	Preparatory Rudiments Exams Set #2
GP - EPS2A	ISBN: 978-1-927641-09-5	Preparatory Exams Answers Set #2
GP - EBS1	ISBN: 978-1-927641-02-6	Basic Rudiments Exams Set #1
GP - EBS1A	ISBN: 978-1-927641-10-1	Basic Exams Answers Set #1
GP - EBS2	ISBN: 978-1-927641-03-3	Basic Rudiments Exams Set #2
GP - EBS2A	ISBN: 978-1-927641-11-8	Basic Exams Answers Set #2
GP - EIS1	ISBN: 978-1-927641-04-0	Intermediate Rudiments Exams Set #1
GP - EIS1A	ISBN: 978-1-927641-12-5	Intermediate Exams Answers Set #1
GP - EIS2	ISBN: 978-1-927641-05-7	Intermediate Rudiments Exams Set #2
GP - EIS2A	ISBN: 978-1-927641-13-2	Intermediate Exams Answers Set #2
GP - EAS1	ISBN: 978-1-927641-06-4	Advanced Rudiments Exams Set #1
GP - EAS1A	ISBN: 978-1-927641-14-9	Advanced Exams Answers Set #1
GP - EAS2	ISBN: 978-1-927641-07-1	Advanced Rudiments Exams Set #2
GP - EAS2A	ISBN: 978-1-927641-15-6	Advanced Exams Answers Set #2

Ultimate Music Theory Supplemental Exam Series

GP-L5E	ISBN: 978-1-990358-11-1	LEVEL 5 Exams
GP-L5EA	ISBN: 978-1-990358-12-8	LEVEL 5 Exams Answers
GP-L6E	ISBN: 978-1-990358-13-5	LEVEL 6 Exams
GP-L6EA	ISBN: 978-1-990358-14-2	LEVEL 6 Exams Answers
GP-L7E	ISBN: 978-1-990358-15-9	LEVEL 7 Exams
GP-L7EA	ISBN: 978-1-990358-16-6	LEVEL 7 Exams Answers
GP-L8E	ISBN: 978-1-990358-17-3	LEVEL 8 Exams
GP-L8EA	ISBN: 978-1-990358-18-0	LEVEL 8 Exams Answers

Go to UltimateMusicTheory.com and check out the FREE Resources

Ultimate Music Theory FREE RESOURCES created just for you!

Ultimate Music Theory
LEVEL 7 Supplemental Exams

Table of Contents

Ultimate Music Theory: *The Way to Score Success!*

The 2016 RCM Theory Syllabus has added the Level 7 Theory Examination, to be completed after the Level 6 Theory Exam (formerly the Intermediate Rudiments Exam), and covers:

♫ **All Concepts introduced in the Ultimate Music Theory Intermediate Workbook.**

♫ **All New Concepts introduced in the Level 6 Supplemental Workbook PLUS:**

♫ **Pitch and Notation:** Transposition of melodies up **or down** by any interval or to any key.

♫ **Rhythm and Meter:** Double dotted notes and rests.

♫ **Intervals:** All intervals above **or below** a given note within an octave.

♫ **Chords and Harmony**: Triads built on any degree of a Major or minor (harmonic) scale using Functional Chord Symbols and Root/Quality Chord Symbols.
   - Leading-Tone Diminished 7th Chords in minor keys, Root Position only, using Functional Chord Symbols (vii°7) and Root/Quality Chord Symbols (E°7).
   - Dominant 7th Chords and their inversions, using Functional Chord Symbols and Root/Quality Chord Symbols.
   - Identification **and writing** of Authentic and Half Cadences on a Grand Staff, using Root Position Chords in Major and minor keys, in Keyboard Style.

♫ **Melody and Composition**: Melodic Passing and Neighbor Tones (unaccented only), within a harmonic context of I, IV and V (Major keys) or i, iv and V (minor keys).
   - Composition of a Contrasting Period in a Major Key, given the Antecedent Phrase.

♫ **Form and Analysis**: Application of Functional or Root/Quality Chord Symbols to a melody, using Root Position I, IV and V Chords (Major keys) or i, iv and V Chords (minor keys), maintaining a harmonic rhythm of one chord per measure.

♫ **Musical Terms and Signs**: New Terms and Signs have been added.

♫ **Music History**: Introduction to Musical Styles of the Romantic and Modern Eras. "Overture to A Midsummer Night's Dream"; "Etude in c minor, opus 10, no. 12" ("Revolutionary"); "Petrushka"; "Dripsody"; and "Ko-Ko". (To include Composer, Genre, Performing Forces and Style Traits.)

Study and Memorize the UMT Map - LEVEL 7

Circle of Fifths

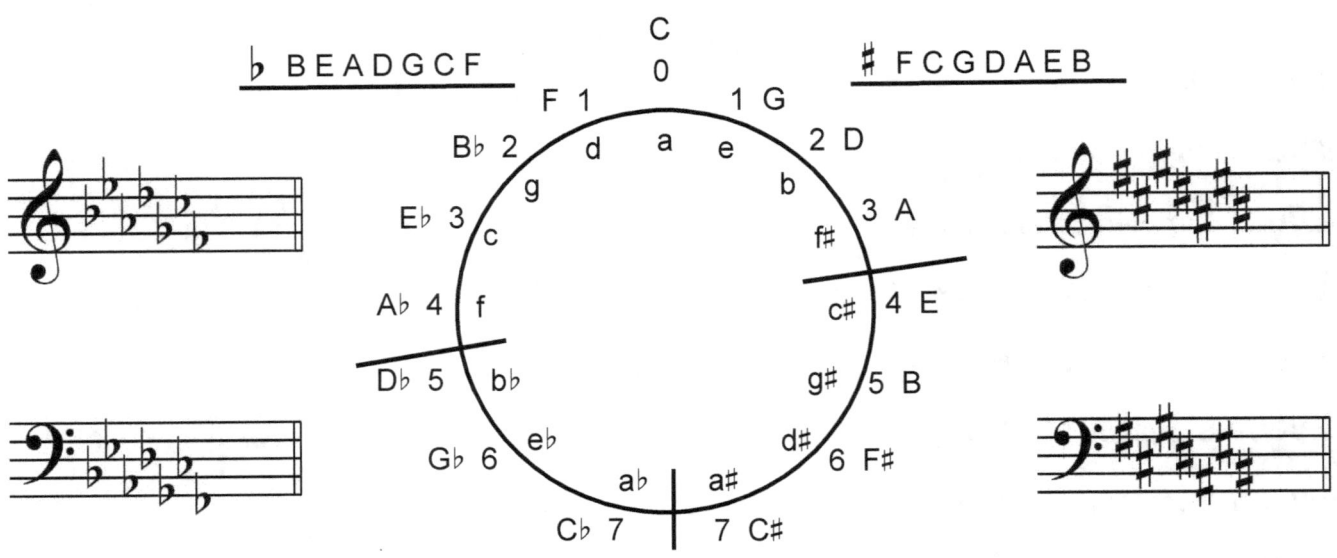

♭ B E A D G C F

♯ F C G D A E B

Key	Chord Root	Quality	Root/Quality	Functional Chord	Inversion Symbols			
E Major	A	Major	A	IV	IV	IV^6	IV$^6_4$	
e minor	A	minor	Am	iv	A	A/C♯	A/E	
e minor	G	Augmented	G+ or Gaug	III+				
E Maj / e min	B	Dominant 7th	B7	V7	V^7	V$^6_5$	V$^4_3$	V$^4_2$
e minor	D♯	diminished	D♯° or D♯dim	vii°	B7	B7/D♯	B7/F♯	B7/A
e minor	D♯	diminished 7th	D♯°7 or D♯dim7	vii°7				

"Irregular Group"	Simple Time	Compound Time
⌐—2—⌐		2 = 3
⌐—3—⌐	3 = 2	
⌐—4—⌐		4 = 3
⌐—5—⌐	5 = 4	5 = 3 or 5 = 6
⌐—6—⌐	6 = 4	
⌐—7—⌐	7 = 4	7 = 3 or 7 = 6

# of Notes: (+ Upper Tonic)	Ti-Do Tip:	Type of Scale:
6 notes	1st interval: Major 2	Major pentatonic
6 notes	1st interval: minor 3	minor pentatonic
7 notes	7 different notes	Whole Tone scale
7 notes	$\hat{4}$ or $\hat{5}$ twice	Blues scale
8 notes	Major or minor (natural, harmonic or melodic)	
9 notes	Alternate HS & WS	Octatonic scale
13 notes	All half steps	Chromatic scale

Melody Writing

Parallel Period: a + a1

Contrasting Period: a + b

Stable Scale Degrees: $\hat{1}$ and $\hat{3}$

Unstable Scale Degrees: $\hat{2}$ and $\hat{7}$

Exam Tip: Copy the UMT Map for LEVEL 7 below. Using a blank piece of paper, write out the UMT Map from memory before beginning each practice exam and the final exam.

Circle of Fifths

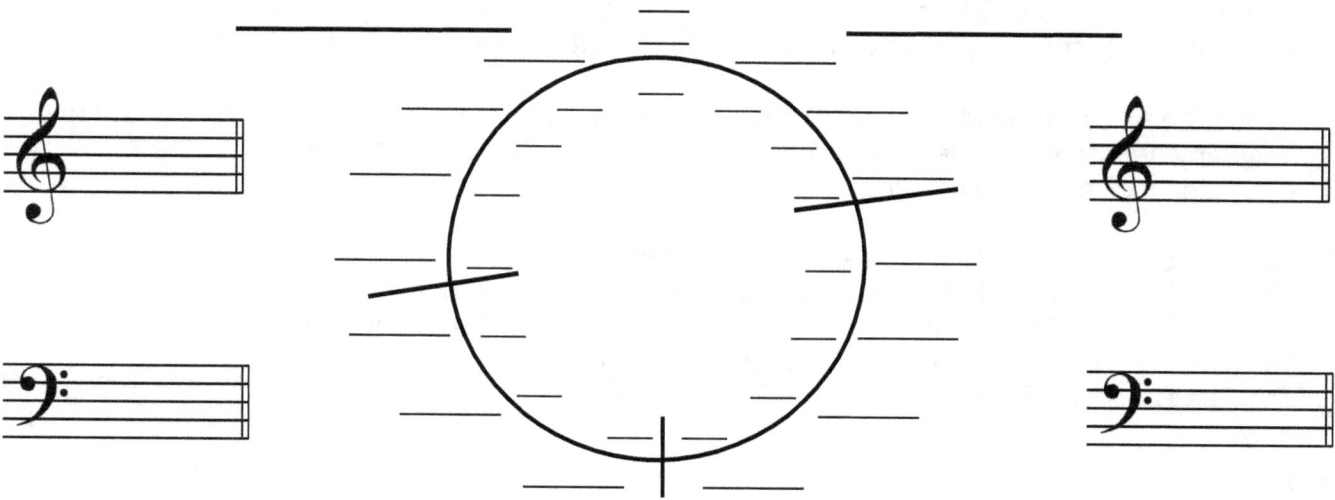

Key	Chord Root	Quality	Root/Quality	Functional Chord	Inversion Symbols		
E Major	A	Major	____	IV	IV IV⁶ IV⁶₄		
e minor	A	minor	____	iv	A ____ ____		
e minor	G	Augmented	____ or ____	III+			
E Maj / e min	B	Dominant 7th	____	V7	V⁷	V⁶₅	V⁴₃ V⁴₂
e minor	D♯	diminished	____ or ____	vii°	B7 ____ ____		
e minor	D♯	diminished 7th	____ or ____	vii°7			

"Irregular Group"	Simple Time	Compound Time
⌐²¬		__ = __
⌐³¬	__ = __	
⌐⁴¬		__ = __
⌐⁵¬	__ = __	__ = __ or __ = __
⌐⁶¬	__ = __	
⌐⁷¬	__ = __	__ = __ or __ = __

# of Notes: (+ Upper Tonic)	Ti-Do Tip:	Type of Scale:
6 notes	1st interval: Major 2	
6 notes	1st interval: minor 3	
7 notes	7 different notes	
7 notes	$\hat{4}$ or $\hat{5}$ twice	
8 notes		
9 notes	Alternate HS & WS	
13 notes	All half steps	

Melody Writing

Parallel Period: ____ + ____

Contrasting Period: ____ + ____

Stable Scale Degrees: ____ and ____

Unstable Scale Degrees: ____ and ____

Ultimate Music Theory
LEVEL 7 Supplemental Exam #1

Total Score: _____
100

The Ultimate Music Theory™ Intermediate Rudiments Workbook, LEVELS 6 & 7 Supplemental Workbooks, Intermediate Rudiments Exam Series and Level 7 Supplemental Exams prepare students for successful completion of the Royal Conservatory of Music Level 7 Theory Examination.

1. Write the following Solid (Blocked) Triads or Chords. Use whole notes. Use a Key Signature and any necessary accidentals. Write the Root/Quality Chord Symbol above and the Functional Chord Symbol below.

10
a) The Supertonic Triad of D Major, in second inversion.
b) The Subdominant Triad of d minor, harmonic form, in first inversion.
c) The Leading Tone Triad of e flat minor, harmonic form, in root position.
d) The Mediant Triad of A Major, in second inversion.
e) The Dominant Seventh Chord of E Major, in third inversion.

Root/Quality
Chord Symbol: a) _____ b) _____ c) _____ d) _____ e) _____

Functional
Chord Symbol: a) _____ b) _____ c) _____ d) _____ e) _____

2. Write the following harmonic interval below each of the given notes. Use whole notes.

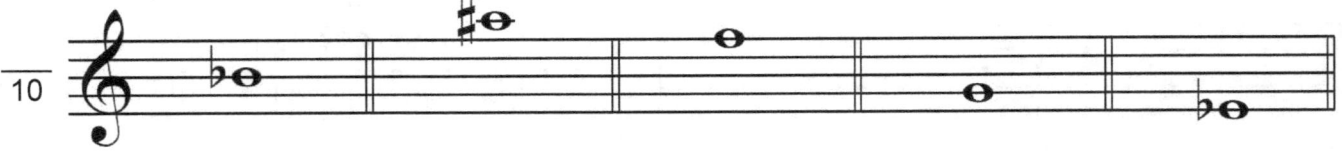

10

Perfect 8   Augmented 6   Major 7   minor 3   diminished 4

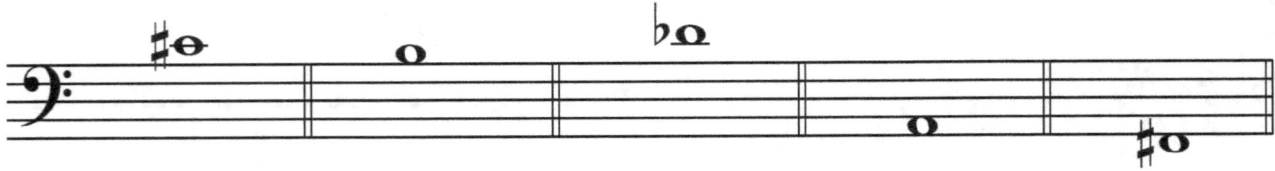

Major 3   Perfect 4   Major 2   minor 7   Augmented 5

3. a) Name the key of this melody.
    b) Compose a four-measure Answer phrase to create a **Contrasting** Period. End on a stable scale degree. (There will be more than one correct answer.)
    c) Draw a phrase mark over the Question (Antecedent) phrase and over the contrasting Answer (Consequent) phrase.
    d) Label the type of cadence (Authentic or Half) at the end of each phrase.

___
10

Key: _____   Cadence: _____

Cadence: _____

4. Match each musical term or sign with the English definition. (Not all definitions will be used.)

___
10

Term		Definition
agitato	c	a) resolute
giocoso	___	b) above
martellato	___	c̶) agitated
morendo	___	d) two octaves higher
risoluto	___	e) sad
semplice	___	f) strongly accented, hammered
sopra	___	g) lively
tutti	___	h) one octave higher
vivo	___	i) humorous, jocose
dolente	___	j) simple
quindicesima alta, 15ma	___	k) a passage for the ensemble
		l) dying, fading away

5. Answer the following questions.

    a) Name the composer of "Dripsody".

10 _____

    b) Name the composer of the "Overture to A Midsummer Night's Dream".

    _____

    c) Name the composer of "Ko-Ko".

    _____

    d) Name the composer of "Petrushka".

    _____

    e) Name the composer of "Etude in c minor, opus 10, number 12".

    _____

    f) Name the type of instrumental music with a descriptive title based on a literary idea.

    _____

    g) Name the type of music that is a single-movement concert piece for an orchestra.

    _____

    h) Name the musical structure used in Jazz that is based upon the I, IV and V chords.

    _____

    i) Name the genre of music that is produced or modified by devices such as synthesizers.

    _____

    j) Name the genre of music that is non-verbal storytelling through choreography performed to music.

    _____

6.   Add rests below the brackets to complete each of the following measures.

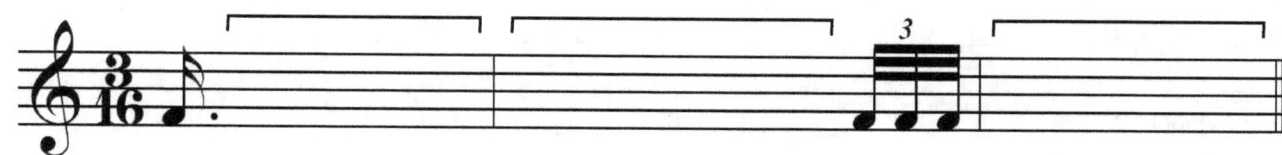

7.   The following melody is in the key of B flat Major.

   a) Transpose the given melody down a Perfect fourth in the same clef. Use the correct Key
      Signature. Name the new key.

Key: _____

   b) Transpose the given melody up into the key of D Major in the same clef. Name the interval
      of transposition.

Interval of Transposition: _____

8. For each of the following Seventh Chords:

    a) Name the key.
    b) Label the chord using a Functional Chord Symbol.

10

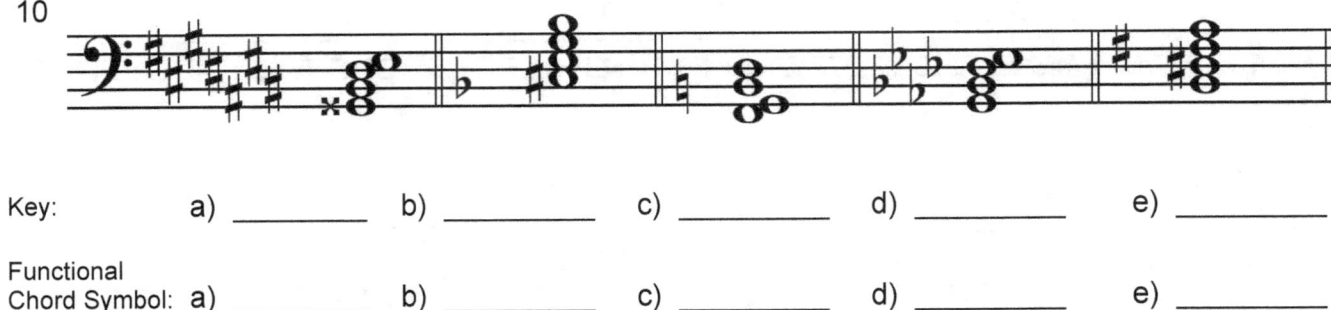

Key: a) _____   b) _____   c) _____   d) _____   e) _____

Functional
Chord Symbol: a) _____   b) _____   c) _____   d) _____   e) _____

9. For each of the following excerpts:

    a) Name the key.
    b) Write the Root/Quality Chord Symbol (root position) implied by the melody on the line above.
    c) Write the Functional Chord Symbol (root position) implied by the melody on the line below.
10 d) Circle and label any passing tones as pt. Circle and label any neighbor tones as nt.

Root/Quality
Chord Symbol: _____   _____   _____   _____

Key: _____

Functional
Chord Symbol: _____   _____   _____   _____

Root/Quality
Chord Symbol: _____   _____   _____   _____

Key: _____

Functional
Chord Symbol: _____   _____   _____   _____

10. Analyze this excerpt from Julianne Warkentin's arrangement of "King Wenceslas Stomp" by answering the questions below.

a) For the triad at letter **A**, identify: Root: _____ Quality: _____ Position: _____

b) For the triad at letter **B**, identify: Root: _____ Quality: _____ Position: _____

c) Explain the term at letter **C**. _____

d) Explain the sign at letter **D**. _____

e) Explain the term at letter **E**. _____

f) Identify the interval at letter **F**. _____.   Identify the interval at letter **G**. _____.

g) Explain the sign at letter **H**. _____

h) Explain the sign at letter **I**. _____

i) Explain the sign at letter **J**. _____

j) Add the missing rests at letter **K**.

Ultimate Music Theory
LEVEL 7 Supplemental Exam #2

Total Score: _____
100

1. For each of the following excerpts:

   a) Name the key.
   ___ b) Write the Root/Quality Chord Symbol (root position) implied by the melody on the line above.
   10 c) Write the Functional Chord Symbol (root position) implied by the melody on the line below.
   d) Circle and label any passing tones as pt. Circle and label any neighbor tones as nt.

Root/Quality
Chord Symbol: _____   _____   _____   _____

Key: _____

Functional
Chord Symbol: _____   _____   _____   _____

Root/Quality
Chord Symbol: _____   _____   _____   _____

Key: _____

Functional
Chord Symbol: _____   _____   _____   _____

2. Write one note or one rest that equals the total value of the notes or rests when added together.

___
10
a) 𝄻 + 𝄽 + 𝄽 = _____   b) o + 𝅗𝅥 + 𝅗𝅥 = _____

c) ♪ + ♪ + ♪ = _____   d) 𝄽 + 𝄾 + 𝄾 = _____

e) 𝄾 + 𝄾 + 𝄾 = _____   f) o + 𝅗𝅥 + ♩ = _____

g) 𝄻 + 𝄼 + 𝄽 = _____   h) ♩ + ♩ + ♩ = _____

i) ♩ + ♪ + ♪ = _____   j) 𝄻 + 𝄼 + 𝄼 = _____

3. a) Write the following melodic interval below each of the given notes. Use whole notes.

10

      minor 6   Major 2   Augmented 5   Perfect 4   diminished 3

   b) Invert the above intervals in the same clef. Name the inversions.

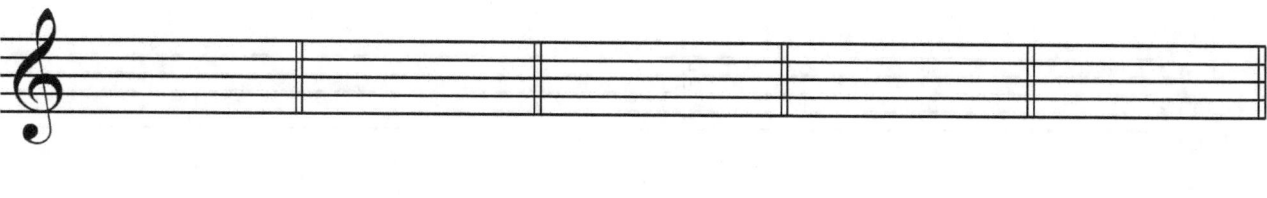

   _____   _____   _____   _____   _____

4. Add the correct Time Signature below each bracket to complete the following rhythms.

10

5. Write the following Solid (Blocked) Chords. Use whole notes. Use a Key Signature and any necessary accidentals. Write the Root/Quality Chord Symbol above and the Functional Chord Symbol below.

10
   a) The Dominant Seventh Chord of b flat minor in first inversion.
   b) The Dominant Seventh Chord of B flat Major in third inversion.
   c) The Leading-Tone Diminished Seventh Chord of e minor in root position.
   d) The Dominant Seventh Chord of g sharp minor in second inversion.
   e) The Leading-Tone Diminished Seventh Chord of f minor in root position.

Root/Quality
Chord Symbol: a) _____   b) _____   c) _____   d) _____   e) _____

Functional
Chord Symbol: a) _____   b) _____   c) _____   d) _____   e) _____

6. Circle TRUE or FALSE for each of the following statements.

   a) TRUE or FALSE: The Genre of Mendelssohn's A Midsummer Night's Dream is an Aria.

10 b) TRUE or FALSE: The Form used in A Midsummer Night's Dream is Sonata Form.

   c) TRUE or FALSE: Chopin's Étude Opus 10, No 12 is known as the Revolutionary Étude.

   d) TRUE or FALSE: The Form of Chopin's Étude Op. 10, No. 12 is Ternary Form (ABA1).

   e) TRUE or FALSE: The Genre of Stravinsky's Petrushka is a Ballet.

   f) TRUE or FALSE: The Performing Forces of Petrushka are solo violin and piano.

   g) TRUE or FALSE: The Genre of Le Caine's Dripsody is Electronic Music.

   h) TRUE or FALSE: Le Caine used a Special Purpose Tape Recorder to compose Dripsody.

   i) TRUE or FALSE: The Genre of Duke Ellington's Ko-Ko is Jazz for Big Band.

   j) TRUE or FALSE: The Form (or Musical Structure) of Ko-Ko is 12 Bar Blues.

7. Following the instructions, write the scales ascending and descending. Use whole notes.

a) The Chromatic scale starting on A flat. Use accidentals. Use any standard notation.

10

b) The Whole Tone scale starting on E. Use accidentals. Use any standard notation.

c) The Parallel minor scale, melodic form, of F Sharp Major. Use accidentals.

d) The Enharmonic Tonic minor scale, natural form, of A flat Major. Use a Key Signature.

e) The Enharmonic Relative Major scale of b flat minor. Use a Key Signature.

8. For each of the following melodies:

    a) Name the key of the melody.
    b) Mark the two four-measure phrases with a slur.
    c) Name the type of each Cadence (Authentic or Half).
    d) Circle the correct answer for each question.

    10

Melody #1:

Key: _____   Cadence: _____

Cadence: _____

   i) Melody #1 is an example of: a Parallel Period   or   a Contrasting Period.

Melody #2:

Key: _____   Cadence: _____

Cadence: _____

   ii) Melody #2 is an example of: a Parallel Period   or   a Contrasting Period.

9. a) Provide the name of the new key for each of the following transpositions.

10

Original Key	Interval of Transposition	New Key
D flat Major	Down a diminished fifth	
g sharp minor	Up a Perfect fourth	
E Major	Up a minor second	
f minor	Down a diminished sixth	
G flat Major	Up an Augmented fourth	
a minor	Down a minor third	
e minor	Up a Perfect fifth	
D Major	Down a Major third	
e flat minor	Down a minor seventh	
F Major	Up a Major sixth	

b) Provide the interval (and direction) of transposition for the following pairs of keys.

Original Key	New Key	Interval of Transposition
C Major	Up to D Major	
E flat Major	Up to B Major	
f sharp minor	Down to d sharp minor	
A flat Major	Down to B flat Major	
C flat Major	Up to A Major	
a sharp minor	Up to f minor	
g minor	Down to e flat minor	
F sharp Major	Up to A flat Major	
G Major	Down to C Major	
c minor	Up to f sharp minor	

10. Analyze this excerpt from Variation II of Mozart's 12 Variations on "Ah, Vous Dirai-Je, Maman" by answering the questions below.

a) Name the key of this excerpt. _____

b) Circle a recurrence of the notes (melodic and rhythmic) at letter **A**.

c) For the triad at letter **B**, identify: Root: _____ Quality: _____ Position: _____

d) The triad at letter **B** is the: ☐ Tonic Triad ☐ Subdominant Triad ☐ Dominant Triad.

e) For the triad at letter **C**, identify: Root: _____ Quality: _____ Position: _____

f) Identify the interval at letter **D**. _____. Identify the interval at letter **E**. _____.

g) This excerpt begins on Measure 65. Add the Measure Number in the box at letter **F**.

h) Circle an example of a Whole Step (Whole Tone). Label it as "WS".

i) Circle an example of a Diatonic Half Step (Diatonic Semitone). Label it as "DH".

j) In this excerpt: Identify the number of ties. _____ Identify the number of slurs. _____

Ultimate Music Theory
LEVEL 7 Supplemental Exam #3

Total Score: _____
/ 100

1. For the following melody:

   a) Name the key.
   b) Above the staff, write the Root/Quality Chord Symbol (in root position) outlined by the notes in each measure.
   ___
   /10
   c) Below the staff, write the Functional Chord Symbol (in root position) outlined by the notes in each measure.
   d) Circle and label any passing tones as pt. Circle and label any neighbor tones as nt.

2. Add rests below the brackets to complete each of the following measures.

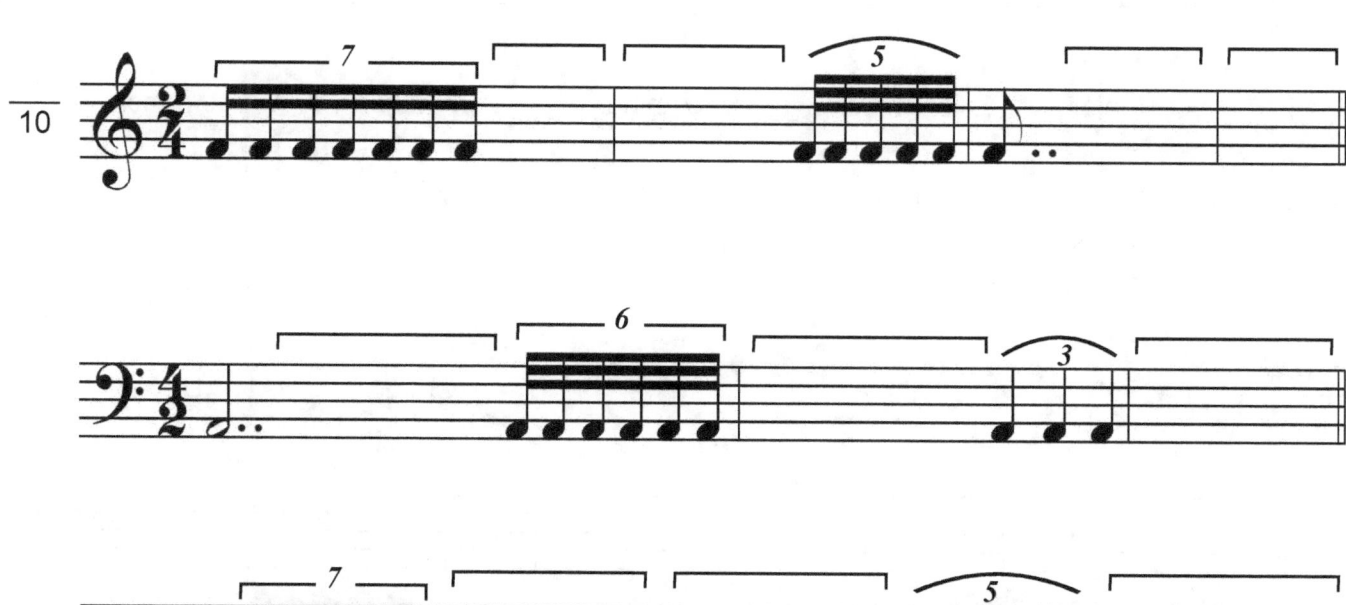

3. For each of the following Dominant Seventh or Leading-Tone Diminished Seventh Chords:

    $\overline{10}$
    a) Name the key.
    b) Write the Root/Quality Chord Symbol above and the Functional Chord Symbol below.

Root/Quality
Chord Symbol: _____   _____   _____   _____   _____

Key: _____   _____   _____   _____

Functional
Chord Symbol: _____   _____   _____   _____

4. Write the following Solid (Blocked) Triads or Chords (in close position). Use a Key Signature and accidentals as needed. Use whole notes.

$\overline{10}$

Key:	C Major	b minor	c# minor	B♭ Major	d minor
Functional Chord Symbol:	iii $\frac{6}{4}$	III+^{6}	vii°	V$\frac{4}{3}$	V$\frac{6}{5}$

Root/Quality Chord Symbol:	G#°/B	D7/F#	E♭+	Cm/G	D#°7

Key:	a minor	G Major	c minor	A♭ Major	e minor

5.　The following melody is in the key of F Sharp Major.

　　a) Transpose the given melody down an Augmented Third in the same clef. Use the correct
　　　 Key Signature. Name the new key.

$\frac{}{10}$

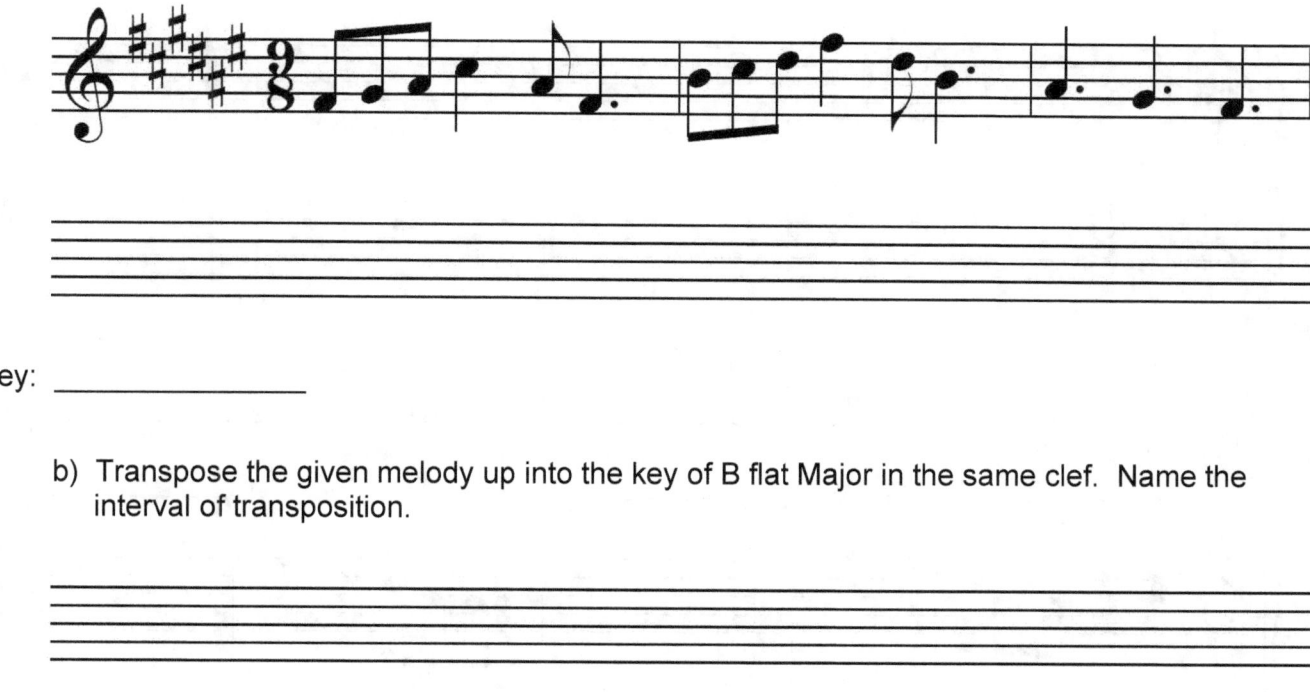

Key: _____

　　b) Transpose the given melody up into the key of B flat Major in the same clef. Name the
　　　 interval of transposition.

Interval of Transposition: _____

6.　Name the following intervals.

$\frac{}{10}$

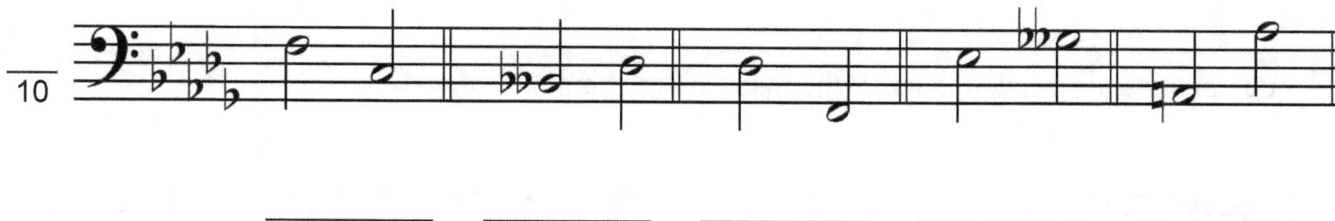

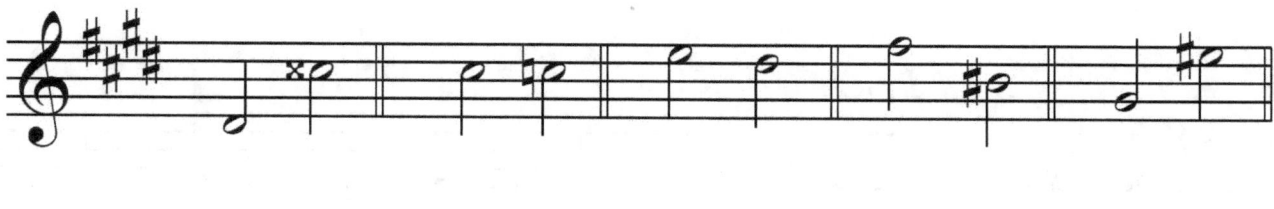

7. a) Name the key.
    b) Write a Cadence in Keyboard Style below the bracketed notes.
    c) Label the chords using Functional Chord Symbols.
    d) Name the type of Cadence (Authentic or Half).

10

Key: _____   ____ ____   ____ ____

Cadence: _____   Cadence: _____

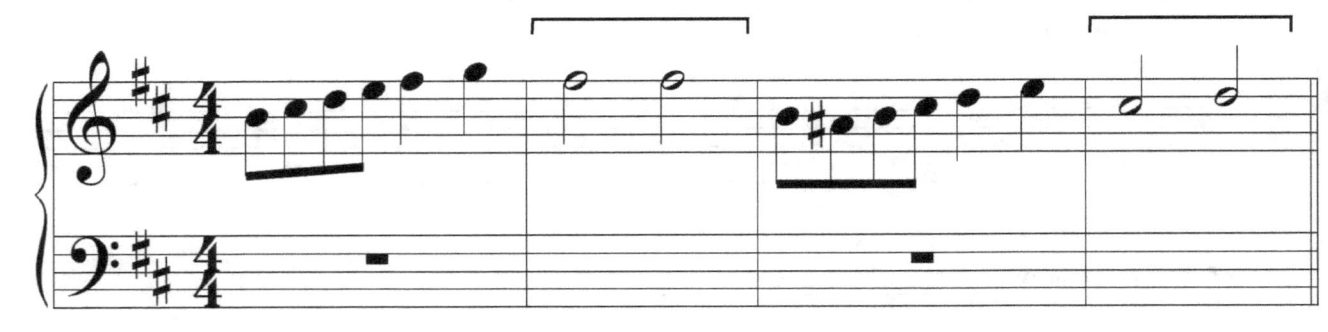

Key: _____   ____ ____   ____ ____

Cadence: _____   Cadence: _____

8. Add bar lines to complete each of the following rhythms.

Ultimate Music Theory
LEVEL 7 Supplemental Exam #3

9. a) Name the following scales as Whole Tone, Octatonic, Major Pentatonic, minor Pentatonic or Blues.

10   i) _____

     ii) _____

     iii) _____

     iv) _____

     v) _____

     vi) _____

b) Write the Chromatic scale starting on B flat, ascending and descending. Use a Key Signature. Use any standard notation. Use whole notes.

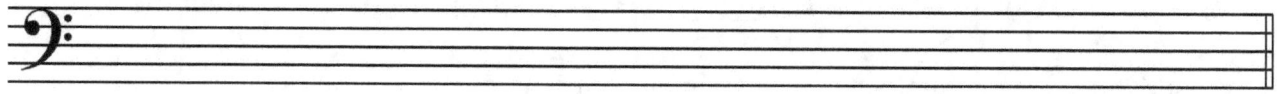

c) Write the Chromatic scale starting on D, ascending and descending. Use accidentals. Use any standard notation. Use whole notes.

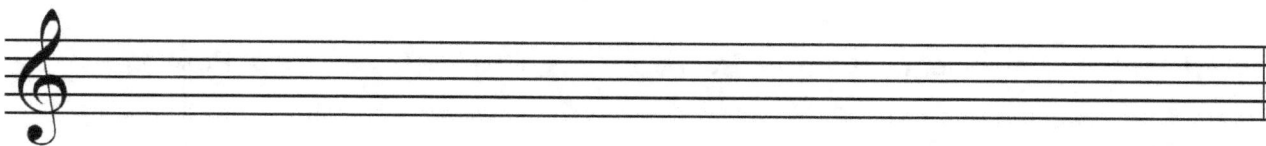

10. Analyze this excerpt from Variation XI of Mozart's 12 Variations on "Ah, Vous Dirai-Je, Maman" by answering the questions below.

Adagio

a) Name the key of this excerpt. _____

b) Explain the sign at letter **A**. _____

c) Circle a recurrence of the notes (melodic and rhythmic) at letter **B** written one octave lower.

d) Explain the sign at letter **C**. _____

e) Identify the interval at letter **D**. _____.   Identify the interval at letter **E**. _____.

f) Add the correct rest at letter **F**.   Name the type of rest. _____

g) Add the correct rest at letter **G**.   Name the type of rest. _____

h) For the triad at letter **H**, identify: Root: _____   Quality: _____   Position: _____

i) For the triad at letter **I**, identify: Root: _____   Quality: _____   Position: _____

j) Identify the cadence at letter **J**: _____

Ultimate Music Theory
LEVEL 7 Supplemental Exam #4

Total Score: _____
100

1. For each of the following Seventh Chords:

   a) Name the key.
   b) Write the Root/Quality Chord Symbol above each Chord.
   _10_ c) Write the Functional Chord Symbol below each Chord.

Root/Quality
Chord Symbol: _____   _____   _____   _____   _____

Key: _____   _____   _____   _____   _____

Functional
Chord Symbol: _____   _____   _____   _____   _____

2. For the following melody:

   a) Name the key.
   b) Above the staff, write the Root/Quality Chord Symbol (in root position) outlined by the notes
   _10_ in each measure.
   c) Below the staff, write the Functional Chord Symbol (in root position) outlined by the notes in
   each measure.
   d) Circle and label any passing tones as pt. Circle and label any neighbor tones as nt.

Root/Quality
Chord Symbol: _____   _____   _____   _____

Key: _____

Functional
Chord Symbol: _____   _____   _____   _____

3. a) Write the following harmonic interval below each of the given notes. Use whole notes.

10

minor 2   Major 7   Augmented 4   diminished 8   Perfect 5

   b) Invert the above intervals in the same clef. Name the inversions.

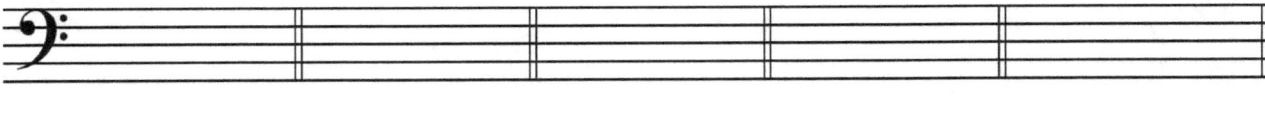

_____   _____   _____   _____   _____

4. a) Name the key.
   b) Write a Cadence in Keyboard Style below the bracketed notes.
   c) Label the chords using Functional Chord Symbols.
   d) Name the type of Cadence (Authentic or Half).

10

Key: _____   _____   _____   _____   _____

          Cadence: _____   Cadence: _____

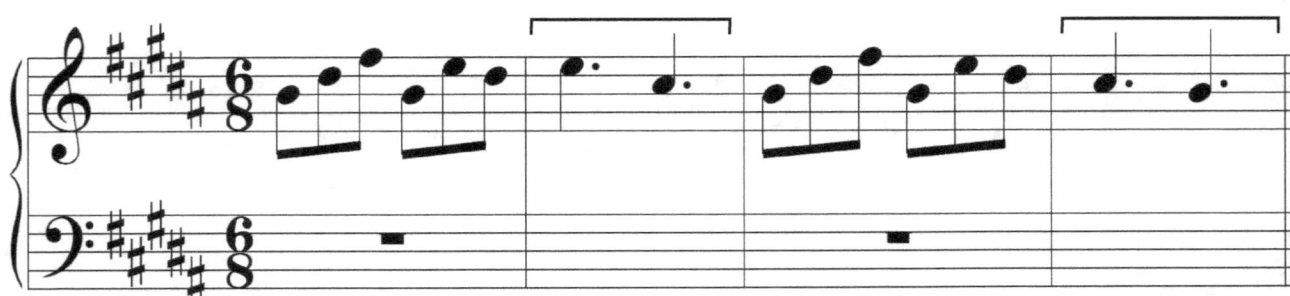

Key: _____   _____   _____   _____   _____

          Cadence: _____   Cadence: _____

5. Write the term or word that each of the following statements applies to. Use the following terms/words (not all terms/words will be used):

___
10

| Polytonality | Petrushka Chord | Concert Overture | Modern Era | Romantic Era |

| Program Music | Jazz | Rondo | Nationalism | Étude | Chromaticism | Rubato |

a) _____ - The use of 2 or more keys sounding simultaneously (at the same time) to create dissonance (tension).

b) _____ - Instrumental music that is given a descriptive title and is written to suggest images or musical ideas for the listener.

c) _____ - The musical period from around 1900 to the present that features innovation, advancement in technology and originality in composition.

d) _____ - The use of musical ideas that are identified with a Composer's Country or Region to show patriotism.

e) _____ - The musical period from around 1825 to 1900 that features freedom of expression and personal feelings in music, poetry and art.

f) _____ - French for "study", this type of composition for solo instrument is written to "study" 1 or 2 specific playing techniques.

g) _____ - A single movement piece for orchestra (often in Sonata Form or a Symphonic Poem Form) that tells a story or describes a scene.

h) _____ - A Polychord of C Major and F sharp Major (a tritone apart) that creates a dissonant sound used to identify the title character of the Ballet.

i) _____ - Music that is a mix or fusion of European musical ideas with African-American styles using syncopation, rhythmic pulse and improvisation.

j) _____ - Greek for "color", this is the use of notes that do not belong to the Key or Key Signature in order to add "color" or dissonance to the harmony.

6. Write the following Solid (Blocked) Triads in the Treble Clef using a Key Signature and any necessary accidentals. Use whole notes. Write the Root/Quality Chord Symbol above the triad and the Functional Chord Symbol below.

10 a) The Supertonic Triad of B flat Major in second inversion.
    b) The Submediant Triad of b minor harmonic form in first inversion.
    c) The Leading Tone Triad of E Major in root position.
    d) The Subdominant Triad of c minor harmonic form in second inversion.
    e) The Mediant Triad of A flat Major in first inversion.

Root/Quality
Chord Symbol: a) _____ b) _____ c) _____ d) _____ e) _____

Functional
Chord Symbol: a) _____ b) _____ c) _____ d) _____ e) _____

7. Match each musical term or sign with the English definition. (Not all definitions will be used.)

Term		Definition
	Term	**Definition**
___	*volti subito, v.s.* _____	a) hammered, strongly accented
10	*con fuoco* _____	b) be silent
	simile _____	c) agitated
	martellato _____	d) turn the page quickly
	risoluto _____	e) sustained
	con grazia _____	f) sad, mournful
	tacet _____	g) with motion
	mesto _____	h) with grace
	con moto _____	i) with fire
	sostenuto _____	j) resolute
		k) continue in the same manner as has just been indicated

8. Add rests below the brackets to complete each of the following measures.

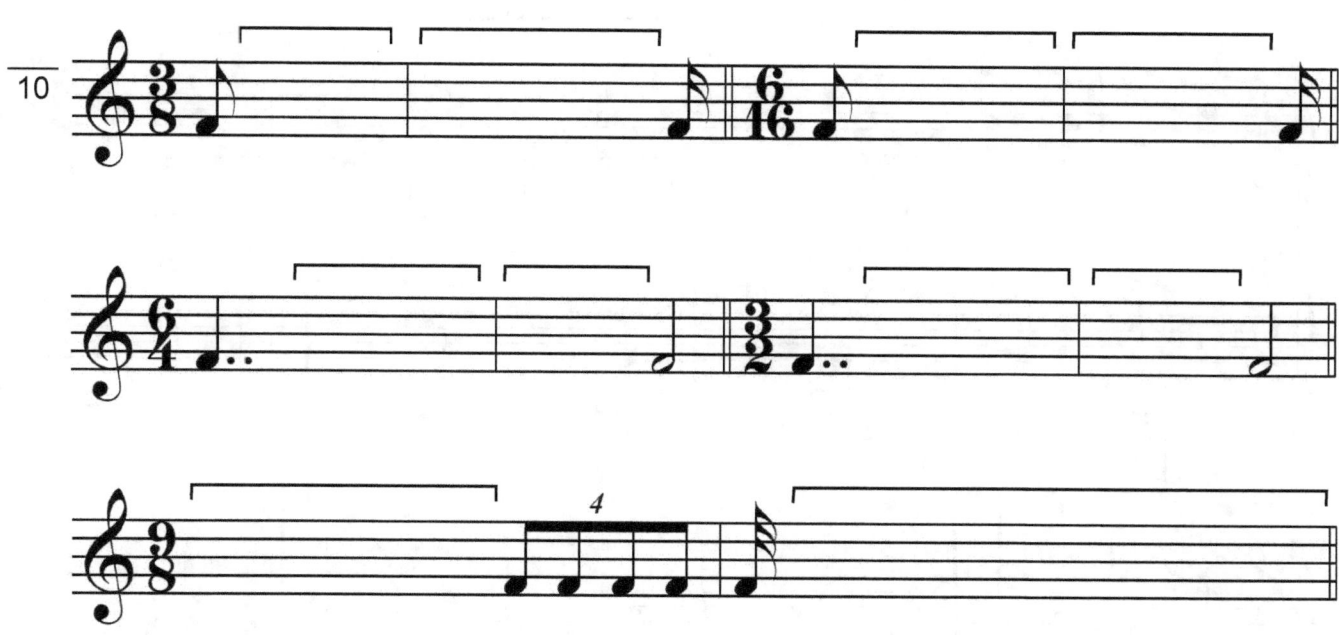

9. a) Name the key of the following melody.

Key: _____

    b) Rewrite the melody at the same pitch. Use a Key Signature and any necessary accidentals.

    c) Transpose the melody down a Major Second in the same clef. Use a Key Signature and any necessary accidentals. Name the new key.

Key: _____

10. Analyze this excerpt from Chopin's Etude in c sharp minor, Opus 25, number 7 by answering the questions below.

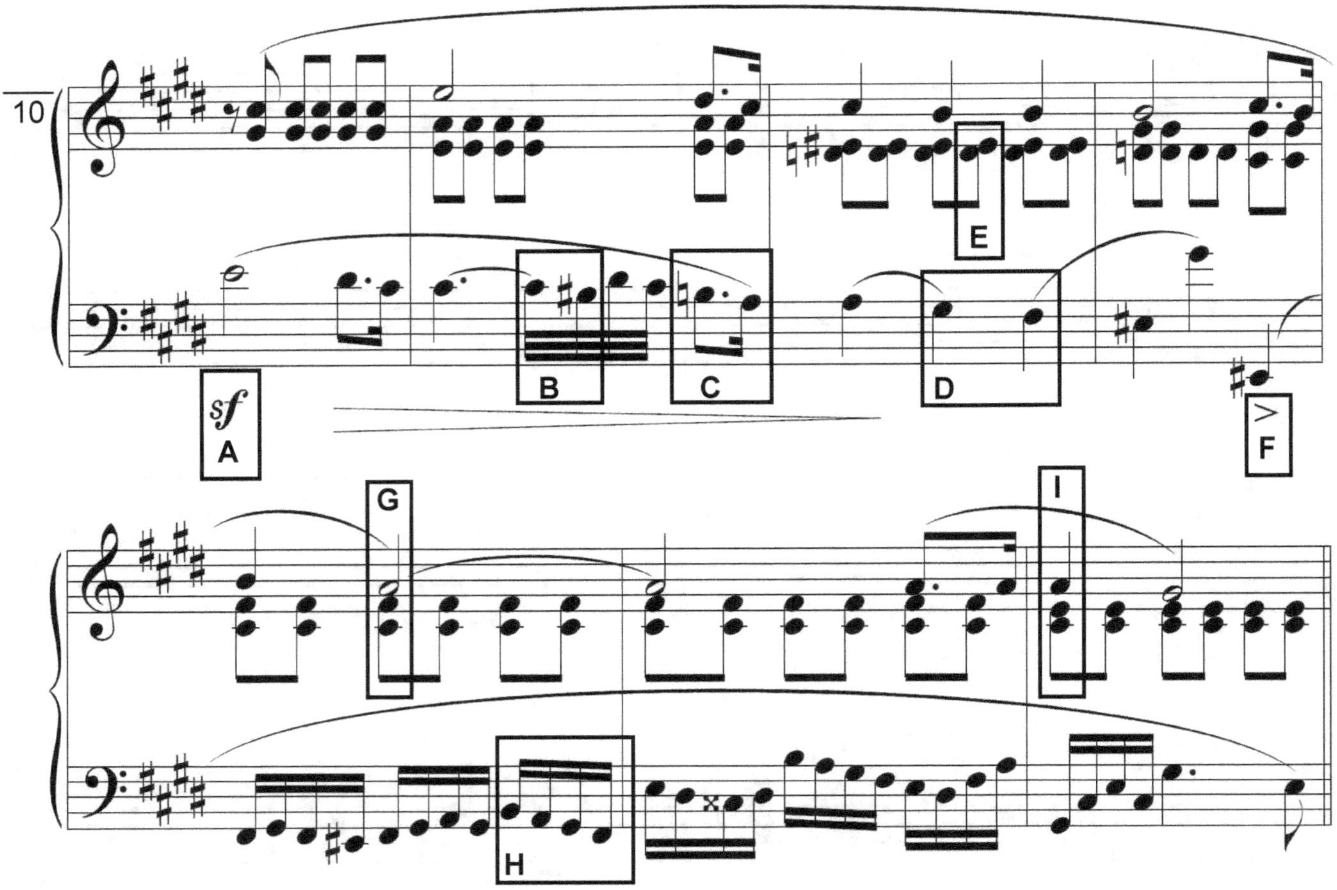

a) Explain the sign at letter **A**. _____

b) Identify the interval at letter **B**. _____.   Identify the interval at letter **C**. _____.

c) Identify the interval at letter **D**. _____.   Identify the interval at letter **E**. _____.

d) Explain the sign at letter **F**. _____

e) For the triad at letter **G**, identify: Root: _____   Quality: _____   Position: _____

f) Circle a recurrence of the notes (melodic and rhythmic) at letter **H** written one octave higher.

g) For the triad at letter **I**, identify: Root: _____   Quality: _____   Position: _____

h) Circle an example of a Whole Step (Whole Tone). Label it as "WS".

i) Circle an example of a Diatonic Half Step (Diatonic Semitone). Label it as "DH".

j) In this excerpt: Identify the number of ties. _____   Identify the number of slurs. _____

Ultimate Music Theory
LEVEL 7 Supplemental Exam #5

Total Score: _____
100

1.   For each of the following Seventh Chords:

___ a) Name the key.
10   b) Write the Root/Quality Chord Symbol above each Chord.
     c) Write the Functional Chord Symbol below each Chord.

Root/Quality
Chord Symbol: _____   _____   _____   _____   _____

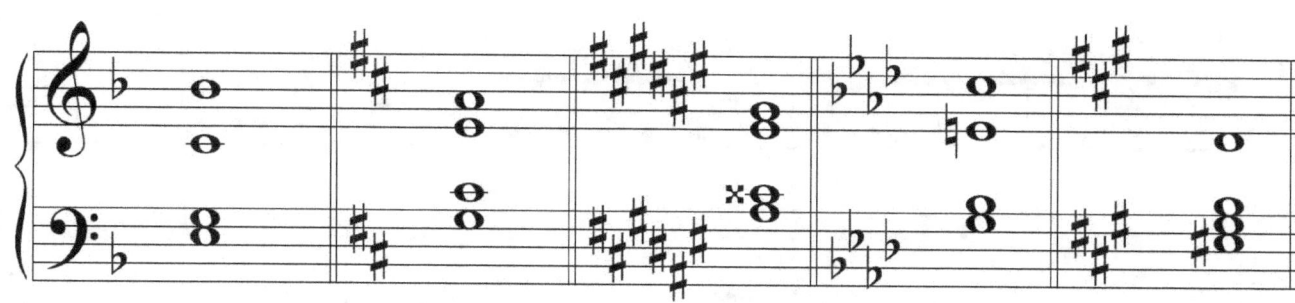

Key: _____   _____   _____   _____   _____

Functional
Chord Symbol: _____   _____   _____   _____   _____

2.   a) Name the key of this melody.
     b) Compose a four-measure Answer phrase to create a **Contrasting** Period. End on a stable
         scale degree. (There will be more than one correct answer.)
___ c) Draw a phrase mark over the Question (Antecedent) phrase and over the contrasting Answer
10   (Consequent) phrase.
     d) Label the type of cadence (Authentic or Half) at the end of each phrase.

Key: _____   Cadence: _____

Cadence: _____

3. Add bar lines to complete the following rhythms.

10

4. Match each musical term or sign with the English definition. (Not all definitions will be used.)

Term		Definition
volta	c	a) be silent
grandioso	___	b) soft, subdued, under the breath
mesto	___	~~c)~~ time
pesante	___	d) with fire
tacet	___	e) playful
sotto voce	___	f) sonorous
scherzando	___	g) grand, grandiose
con fuoco	___	h) weighty, with emphasis
sostenuto	___	i) with grace
sonore	___	j) sad, mournful
con grazia	___	k) with motion
		l) sustained

10

Ultimate Music Theory
LEVEL 7 Supplemental Exam #5

5. a) Name the following intervals.

10

_____ _____ _____ _____ _____

b) Change the upper note of each interval enharmonically. Rename the interval.

_____ _____ _____ _____ _____

6. Identify the work to which each of the following statements applies by writing the appropriate letter (A, B, C, D or E) in the space before each statement.

A - Overture to A Midsummer Night's Dream
B - Étude in c minor, opus 10, number 12
10 C - Petrushka, First Tableau: The Crowd Revels at the Shrovetide Fair
D - Dripsody
E - Ko-Ko

a) _____ This piece is a twelve-bar blues composition with an introduction, 7 choruses and a coda.

b) _____ This piece is to be performed by a virtuosic solo pianist.

c) _____ This piece was composed by a Canadian scientist and physicist.

d) _____ This ballet features polytonality.

e) _____ This piece is written to be performed by a "big band" type of orchestra.

f) _____ The nickname for this piece is "Revolutionary".

g) _____ This piece is an example of 19th Century Program Music.

h) _____ This piece was created using an eyedropper, a metal wastebasket and a tape recorder.

i) _____ The tempo of this piece, which features chromatic harmony, is "*allegro con fuoco*".

j) _____ This piece is an example of Russian Nationalism and includes Russian subjects, folk music and Russian dances.

Ultimate Music Theory
LEVEL 7 Supplemental Exam #5

7. Match each description in the left column with the correct Triad in the right column.

a) The Supertonic Triad of C Major, in first inversion. _____

10

b) The Dominant Triad of C flat Major, in second inversion. _____

c) The Tonic Triad of G flat Major, in root position. _____

d) The Leading Tone Triad of A flat Major, in first inversion. ___a___

e) The Mediant Triad of C sharp Major, in root position. _____

f) The Dominant Triad of f sharp minor harmonic form, in second inversion. _____

g) The Submediant Triad of a sharp minor harmonic form, in first inversion. _____

h) The Subdominant Triad of B flat Major in root position. _____

i) The Supertonic Triad of g sharp minor harmonic form, in first inversion. _____

j) The Subdominant Triad of b flat minor harmonic form, in second inversion. _____

k) The Leading Tone Triad of a minor harmonic form, in second inversion. _____

Ultimate Music Theory
LEVEL 7 Supplemental Exam #5

8. Complete the Transposition Chart by adding in either the missing Interval of Transposition (including the direction) or the missing New Key Name for each of the following.

10

Original Key Name	Interval of Transposition	New Key Name
A flat Major	Up a minor 3	
c sharp minor	Down an Augmented 4	
d minor		Down to g sharp minor
B Major		Up to D flat Major
B flat Major	Down a Major 7	
f minor	Up a Major 6	
d sharp minor		Up to e minor
D flat Major		Down to C flat Major
E Major	Up a Perfect 5	
a minor		Down to e flat minor

9. Rewrite the following rhythms beaming the notes correctly.

10

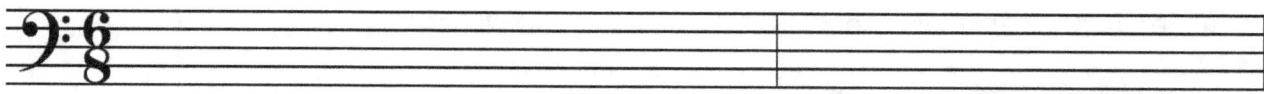

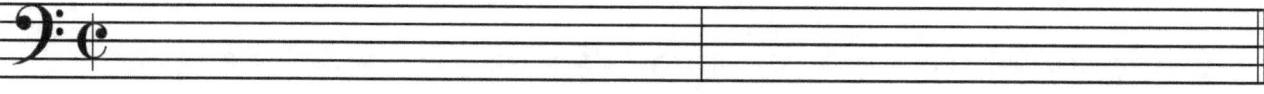

10. Analyze this excerpt from Chopin's Invention No. 9 in f minor by answering the questions below.

Andante con espressione

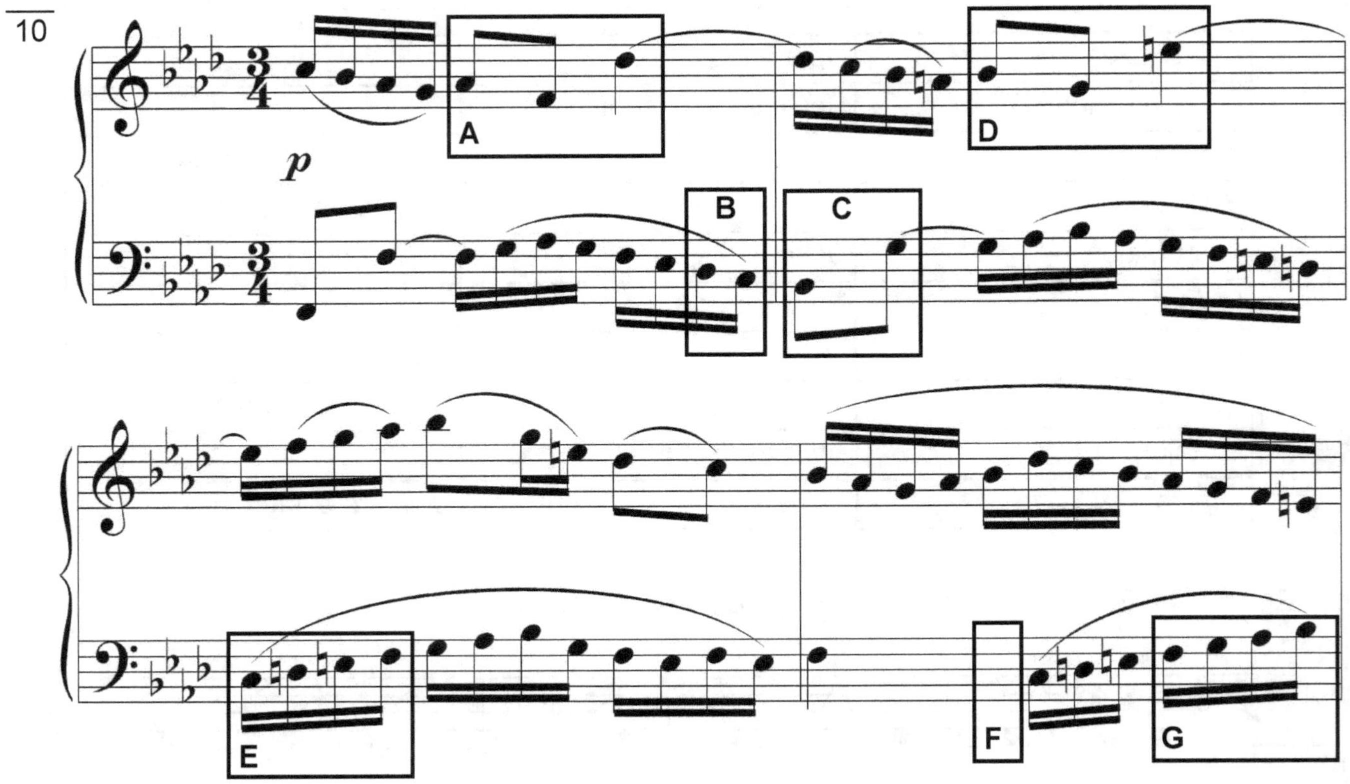

10

a) Explain the tempo. _____

b) For the triad at letter **A**, identify: Root: _____   Quality: _____   Position: _____

c) Identify the interval at letter **B**. _____.   Identify the interval at letter **C**. _____.

d) For the triad at letter **D**, identify: Root: _____   Quality: _____   Position: _____

e) Name the notes (letter names) at letter **E**.   _____ _____ _____ _____

f) Add the correct rest a letter **F**. Name the type of rest used: _____

g) Name the notes (letter names) at letter **G**.   _____ _____ _____ _____

h) Circle an example of a Whole Step (Whole Tone). Label it as "WS".

i) Circle an example of a Diatonic Half Step (Diatonic Semitone). Label it as "DH".

j) In this excerpt: Identify the number of ties. _____   Identify the number of slurs. _____

Ultimate Music Theory
LEVEL 7 Supplemental Exam #6

Total Score: _____
100

1. Write the following Solid (Blocked) Triads or Chords (in close position). Use a Key Signature and accidentals as needed. Use whole notes.

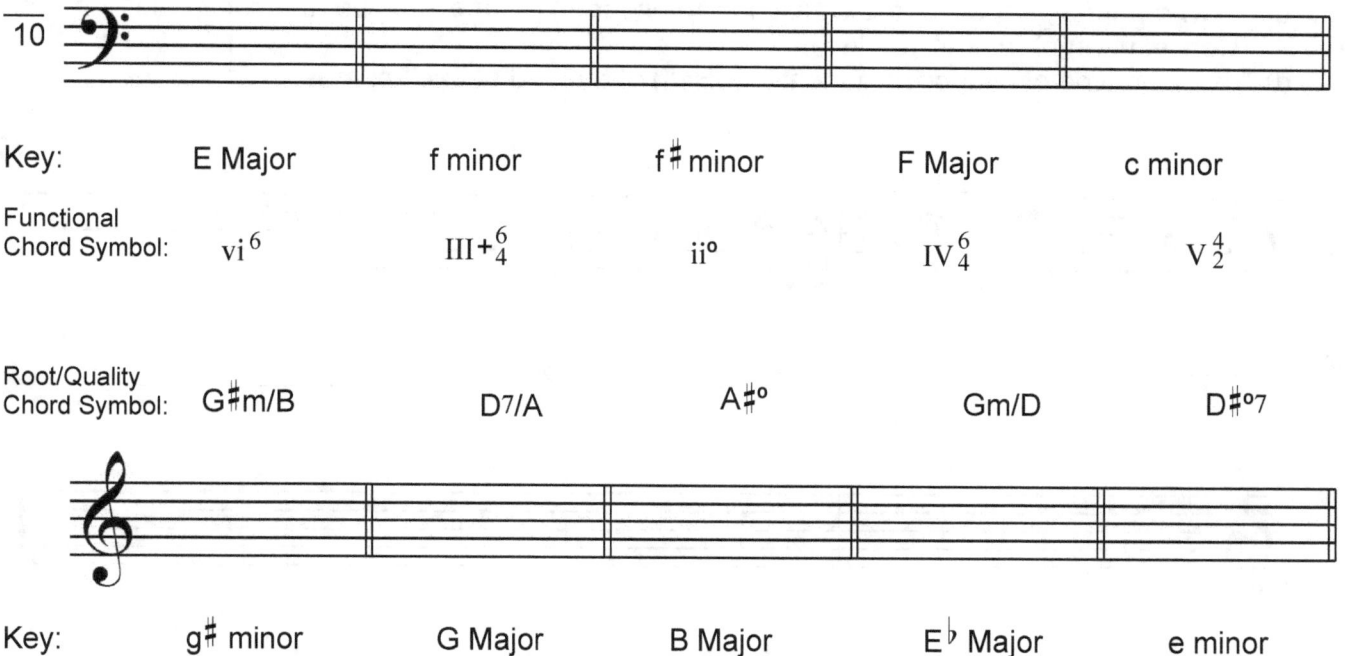

Key:	E Major	f minor	f# minor	F Major	c minor
Functional Chord Symbol:	vi^6	III+$^6_4$	ii^o	IV$^6_4$	V$^4_2$

Root/Quality Chord Symbol:	G#m/B	D7/A	A#^{o}	Gm/D	D#^{o7}

Key:	g# minor	G Major	B Major	E♭ Major	e minor

2. Add Time Signatures to complete the following rhythms.

3. a) Name the key of this melody.
    b) Compose a four-measure Answer phrase to create a **Contrasting** Period. End on a stable scale degree. (There will be more than one correct answer.)
    c) Draw a phrase mark over the Question (Antecedent) phrase and over the contrasting Answer (Consequent) phrase.
    d) Label the type of cadence (Authentic or Half) at the end of each phrase.

___
10

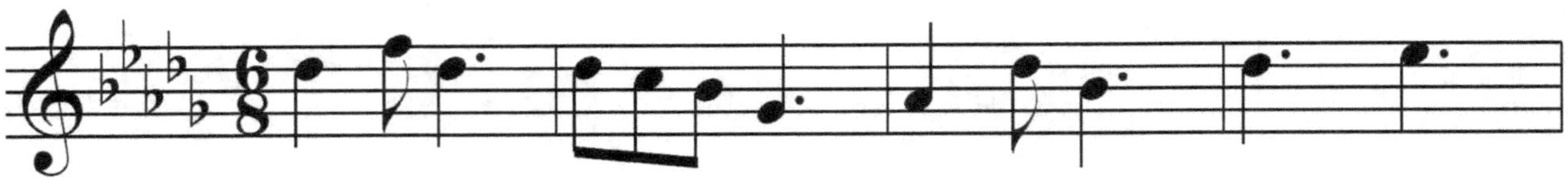

Key: _____   Cadence: _____

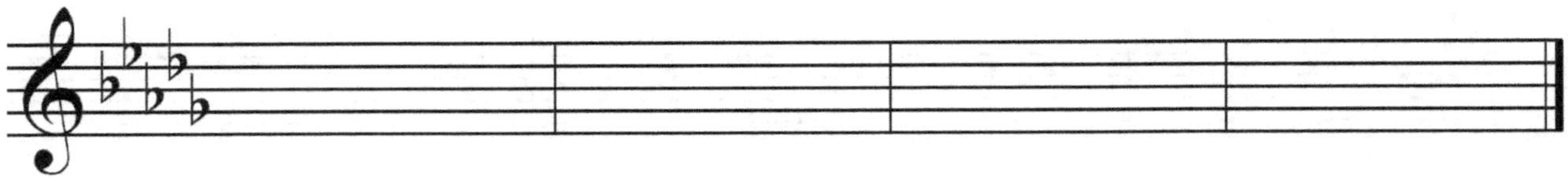

Cadence: _____

4. Write the definition for each of the following terms.

    a) subito forte _____

___
10 b) sotto voce _____

    c) scherzando _____

    d) volti subito _____

    e) quindicesima alta _____

    f) meno mosso _____

    g) ad libitum _____

    h) rubato _____

    i) martellato _____

    j) morendo _____

5. The following melody is in the key of b flat minor.

    a) Transpose the given melody down a diminished 3rd in the same clef. Use the correct Key Signature. Name the new key.

___
10

Key: _____

    b) Transpose the given melody up into the key of e minor in the same clef. Use the correct Key Signature. Name the interval of transposition.

Interval of Transposition: _____

6. a) Write the following harmonic interval below each of the given notes. Use whole notes.

___
10

      Augmented 2   Perfect 4   Major 7   minor 6   diminished 3

    b) Invert the above intervals in the same clef. Name the inversions.

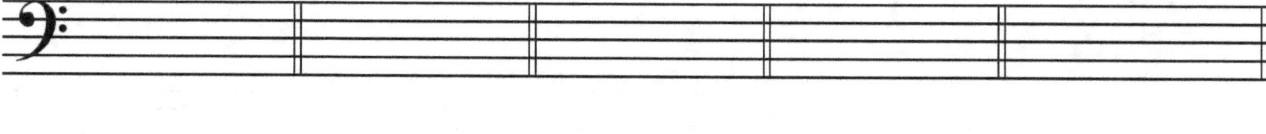

_____   _____   _____   _____   _____

7. Name the following scales as Major, natural minor, harmonic minor, melodic minor, Whole Tone, Chromatic, Major Pentatonic, minor Pentatonic, Blues or Octatonic.

10 a) _____

b) _____

c) _____

d) _____

e) _____

f) _____

g) _____

h) _____

i) _____

j) _____

8.   a)   Name the key of the following melody.

Key: _____

b)   Rewrite the melody at the same pitch. Use a Key Signature and any necessary accidentals.

9.   For each of the following:

a)   Name the key.
b)   Name the type of Cadence (Authentic or Half).

Key: _____   _____

Cadence: _____   _____

Key: _____   _____

Cadence: _____   _____

10. Analyze this excerpt from Variation II of Mozart's 12 Variations on "Ah, Vous Dirai-Je, Maman" by answering the questions below.

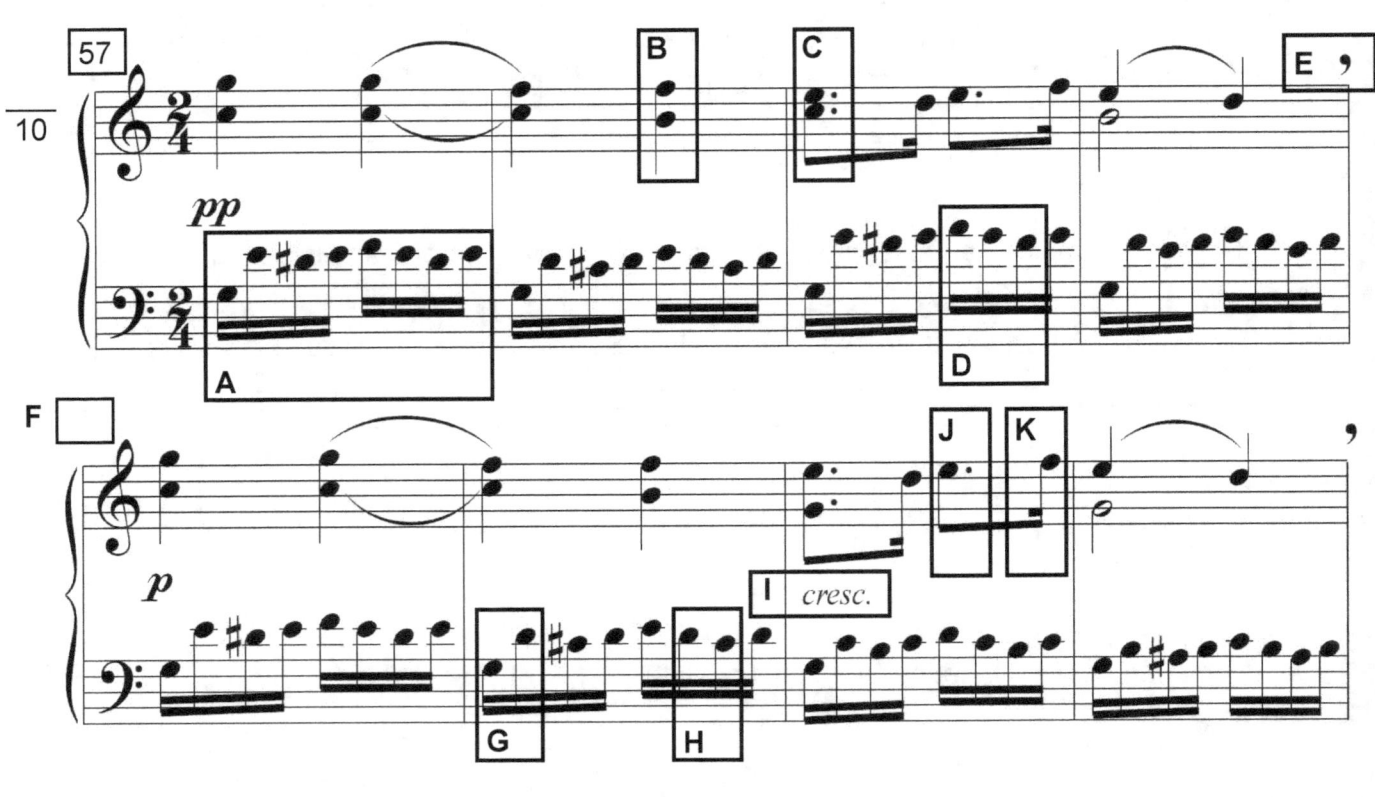

a) Circle a recurrence of the notes (melodic and rhythmic) at letter **A**.

b) Identify the interval at letter **B**. _____ .   Identify the interval at letter **C**. _____ .

c) Identify the letter names of the notes at letter **D**. _____ _____ _____

d) Explain the sign at letter **E**. _____

e) This excerpt begins on Measure 57. Add the correct measure number at letter **F**.

f) Identify the interval at letter **G**. _____ .   Identify the interval at letter **H**. _____ .

g) Explain the sign at letter **I**. _____

h) For the note at letter **J**, identify: Note Name: _____   Type of Note: _____

i) For the note at letter **K**, identify: Note Name: _____   Type of Note: _____

j) In this excerpt, identify the: Number of Ties: _____   Number of Slurs: _____

Ultimate Music Theory
LEVEL 7 Supplemental Exam #7

Total Score: _____
                      100

1. a) Name the following intervals.

_____   _____   _____   _____   _____

   b) Change the lower note of each interval enharmonically. Rename the interval.

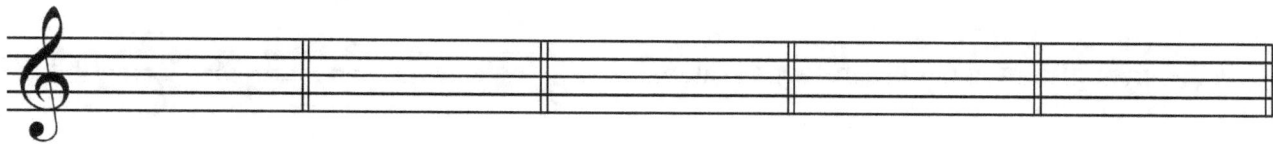

_____   _____   _____   _____   _____

2. a) Name the key.
    b) Write a Cadence in Keyboard Style below the bracketed notes.
    c) Label the chords using Functional Chord Symbols.
    d) Name the type of Cadence (Authentic or Half).

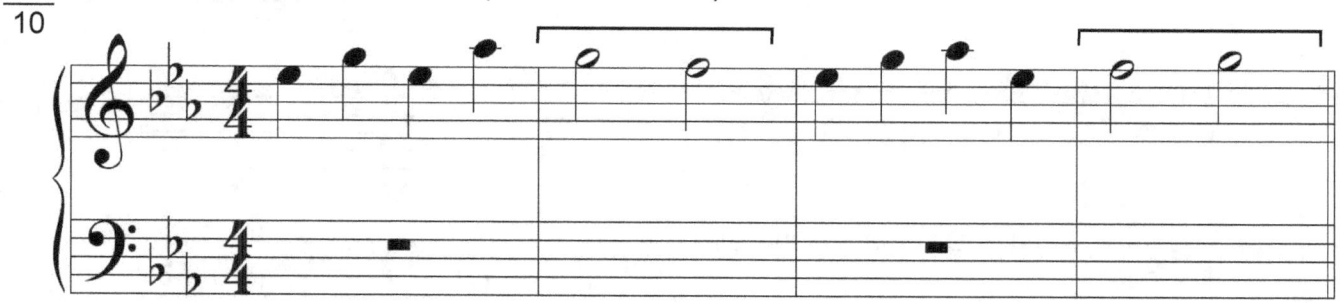

Key: _____   _____ _____   _____ _____

        Cadence: _____   Cadence: _____

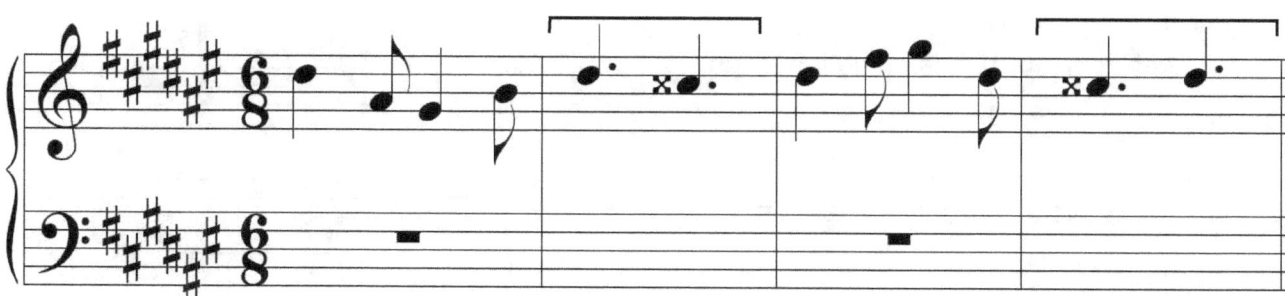

Key: _____   _____ _____   _____ _____

        Cadence: _____   Cadence: _____

3. Match each description in the left column with the correct Chord or Triad in the right column.

    a) The Supertonic Triad of e minor natural form, in first inversion. _____

10

    b) The Subdominant Triad of f minor harmonic form, in second inversion. _____

    c) The Leading Tone Triad of d sharp minor harmonic form, in root position. _____

    d) The Dominant Seventh Chord of G flat Major, in third inversion.   a _____

    e) The Submediant Triad of F sharp Major, in second inversion. _____

    f) The Leading Tone Diminished Seventh Chord of d minor, in root position. _____

    g) The Tonic Triad of D flat Major, in first inversion. _____

    h) The Mediant Triad of b flat minor harmonic form, in root position. _____

    i) The Dominant Seventh Chord of b minor harmonic form, in second inversion. _____

    j) The Dominant Triad of a flat minor harmonic form, in first inversion. _____

    k) The Supertonic Triad of c sharp minor harmonic form, in second inversion. _____

4.   For each of the following Seventh Chords:

    a) Name the key.
    b) Name the type of Chord.

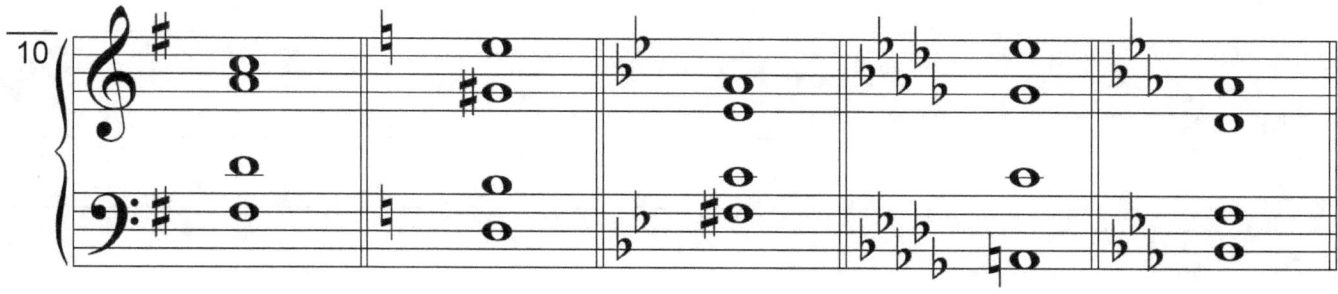

Key: _____   _____   _____   _____   _____

Chord: _____   _____   _____   _____   _____

5.   Fill in the blanks for any ten (10) of the following.

    a) Identify the key of Chopin's "Revolutionary Etude". _____

    b) Identify the Composer of "Dripsody". _____

    c) Identify a Polytonal Ballet by Stravinsky. _____

    d) Identify the Composer of "Overture to a Midsummer Night's Dream". _____

    e) Identify the Era from around 1825 to 1900. _____

    f) Identify the Era from around the 1900 to the current date. _____

    g) Identify the Genre of "Ko-Ko". _____

    h) Identify the type of chord made famous by Stravinsky. _____

    i) Identify the Composer of "Ko-Ko". _____

    j) Identify the Performing Forces for "Ko-Ko". _____

    k) Identify the Genre of "Dripsody". _____

    l) Identify the Performing Forces for the "Revolutionary Etude". _____

6. Identify and explain the following signs.

___
10
a) _____

_____

b) *15ma*¬ _____

_____

c) ⊓ _____

_____

d) , _____

_____

e) V _____

_____

7. For the following melody:

a) Name the key.

___
10
b) Above the staff, write the Root/Quality Chord Symbol (in root position) outlined by the notes in each measure.

c) Below the staff, write the Functional Chord Symbol (in root position) outlined by the notes in each measure.

d) Circle and label any passing tones as pt. Circle and label any neighbor tones as nt.

Root/Quality
Chord Symbol: _____   _____   _____   _____

Key: _____

Functional
Chord Symbol: _____   _____   _____   _____

Ultimate Music Theory
LEVEL 7 Supplemental Exam #7

8. Add rests below the brackets to complete each of the following measures.

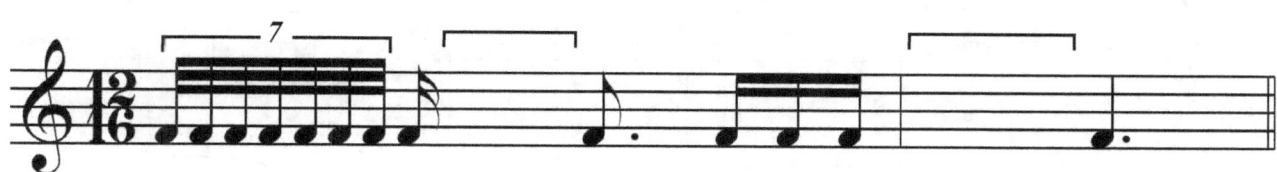

9. Identify the Major or minor key for each of the following.

a) The Tonic minor key of F sharp Major. _____

b) The Enharmonic Relative minor key of C sharp Major. _____

c) The Major key with B as the Dominant note. _____

d) The Enharmonic Tonic Major key of b minor. _____

e) The Relative Major key of e flat minor. _____

f) The minor key with E flat as the Subtonic. _____

g) The Enharmonic Tonic minor key of G flat Major. _____

h) The minor key with G Double Sharp as the Leading Tone. _____

i) The Major key with C as the Supertonic. _____

j) The Tonic Major key of b flat minor. _____

10. Analyze this excerpt from Sly Snake by Julianne Warkentin by answering the questions below.

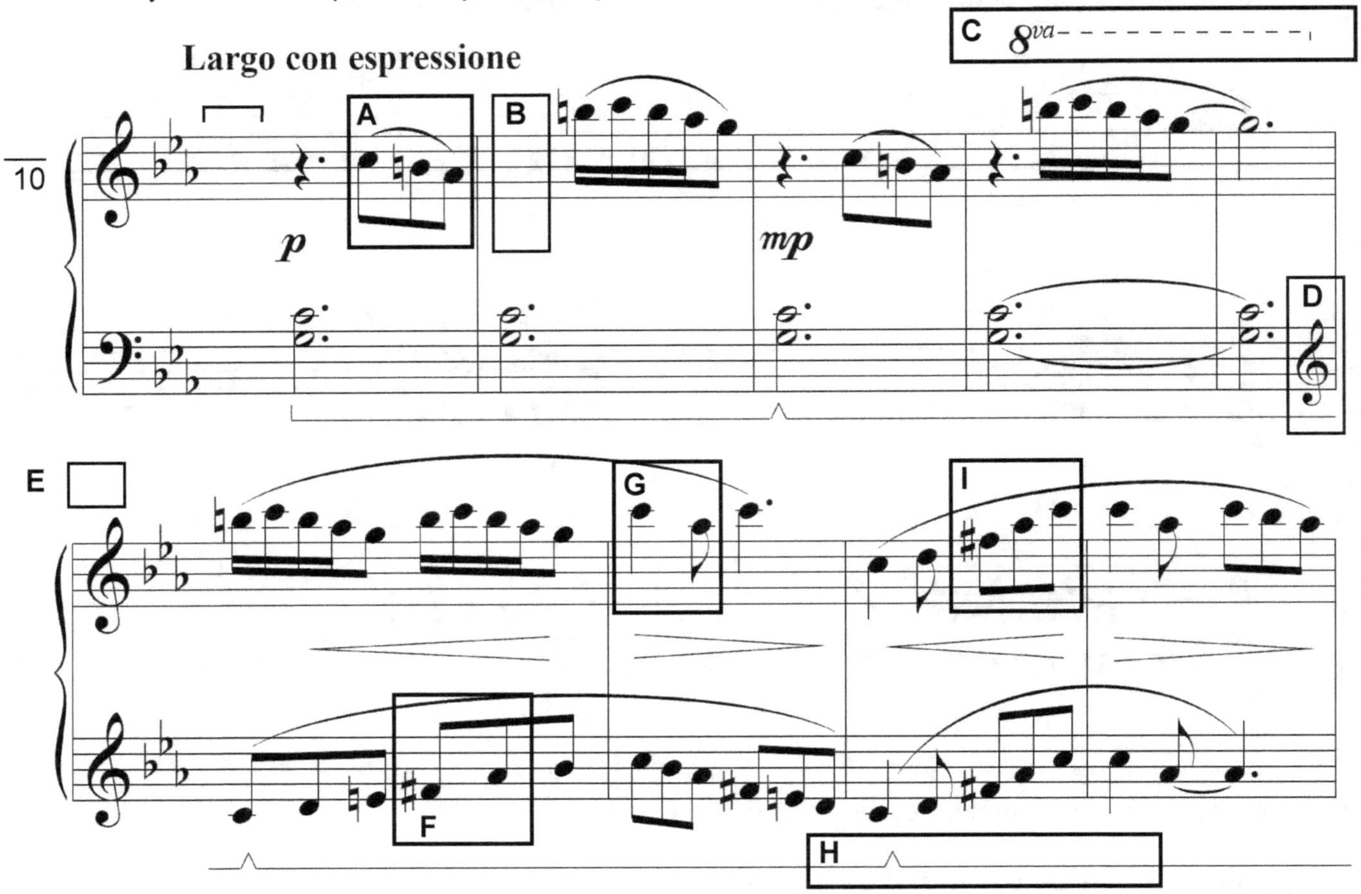

Largo con espressione

a) Write the Time Signature directly on the music.

b) Explain the tempo mark. _____

c) Circle a recurrence of the notes (melodic and rhythmic) at letter **A**.

d) Add the rest at letter **B**. Identify the type of rest used. _____

e) Explain the sign at letter **C**. _____

f) Explain the sign at letter **D**. _____

g) This excerpt begins on Measure 1. Add the correct measure number at letter **E**.

h) Identify the interval at letter **F**. _____.   Identify the interval at letter **G**. _____.

i) Explain the sign at letter **H**. _____

j) Identify the letter names of the notes at letter **I**. _____ _____ _____

Ultimate Music Theory
LEVEL 7 Supplemental Exam #8

Total Score: _____
100

1. a) Name the following intervals.

_____ _____ _____ _____

b) Change the lower note of each interval enharmonically. Rename the interval.

_____ _____ _____ _____

c) Write the following harmonic interval below each of the given notes. Use whole notes.

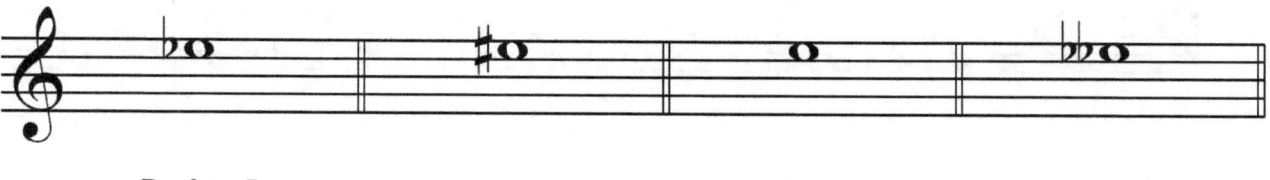

Perfect 5   Augmented 3   minor 6   diminished 7

d) Invert the above intervals in the same clef. Name the inversions.

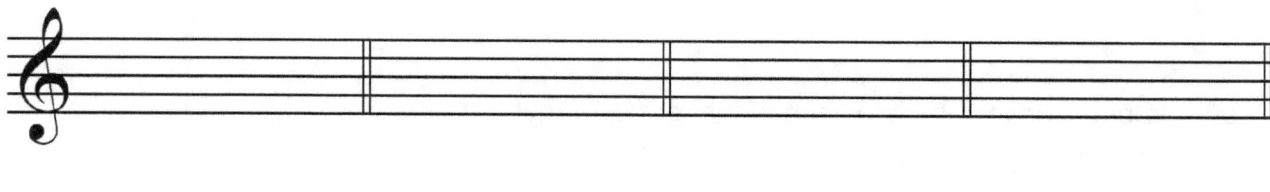

_____ _____ _____ _____

e) Write the following melodic interval above each of the given notes. Use half notes.

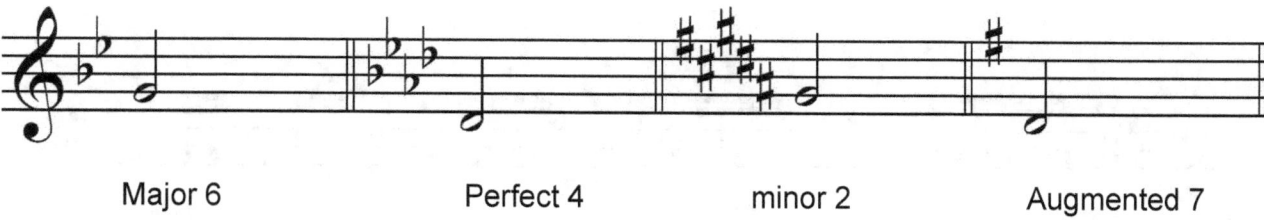

Major 6   Perfect 4   minor 2   Augmented 7

2. a) Add rests below the brackets to complete each of the following measures.

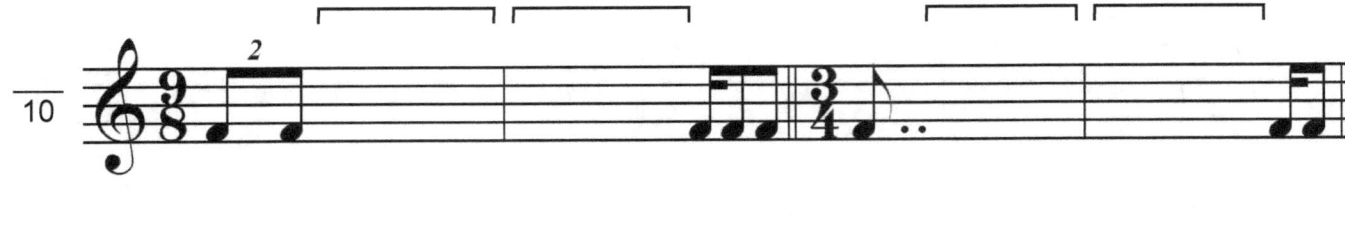

b) Add Time Signatures to complete the following rhythms.

c) Add bar lines to complete each of the following rhythms.

3.   Write the following scales, ascending and descending. Use whole notes.

   a) The Chromatic scale starting on A. Use a Key Signature. Use any standard notation.

‾10‾

   b) The Whole Tone scale starting on D sharp. Use accidentals.

   c) The Major Pentatonic scale starting on E flat. Use a Key Signature.

   d) The Blues scale starting on A. Use accidentals. Use any standard notation.

   e) The minor Pentatonic scale starting on B. Use accidentals.

4.   a) The following melody is in the key of A Major. Transpose the given melody down an
          Augmented 4th in the same clef. Use the correct Key Signature. Name the new key.

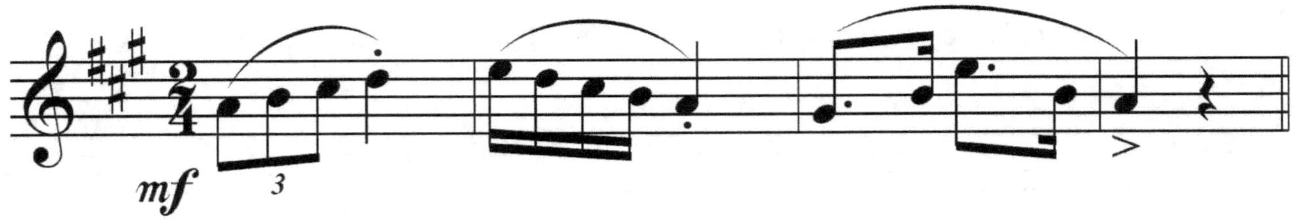

Key: _____

      b) Transpose the given melody up into the key of B Major in the same clef. Name the
          interval of transposition.

Interval of Transposition: _____

      c) Name the key of the following melody.

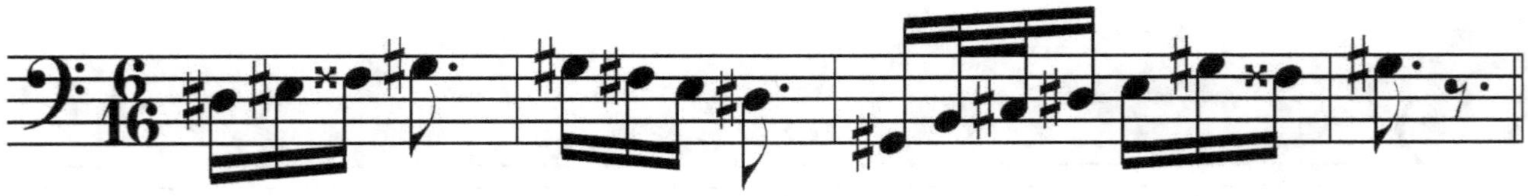

Key: _____

      d) Rewrite the melody at the same pitch. Use a Key Signature and any necessary accidentals.

5. a) Write the following Solid (Blocked) Chords in the Treble Clef using a Key Signature and any necessary accidentals. Use whole notes. Write the Root/Quality Chord Symbol above and the Functional Chord Symbol below.

10 i)   The Dominant Seventh Chord of E Major in second inversion.
     ii) The Supertonic Triad of g minor harmonic form in first inversion.
     iii) The Leading Tone Triad of D Major in root position.
     iv) The Dominant Triad of c sharp minor harmonic form in second inversion.
     v)   The Leading-Tone Diminished Seventh Chord of d minor in root position.

Root/Quality
Chord Symbol: i) _____ ii) _____ iii) _____ iv) _____ v) _____

Functional
Chord Symbol: i) _____ ii) _____ iii) _____ iv) _____ v) _____

b) For each of the following Seventh Chords, name the key. Write the Root/Quality Chord Symbol above each Chord. Write the Functional Chord Symbol below each Chord.

Root/Quality
Chord Symbol: _____   _____   _____   _____   _____

Key: _____   _____   _____   _____   _____

Functional
Chord Symbol: _____   _____   _____   _____   _____

6. a) Name the key.
    b) Write a Cadence in Keyboard Style below the bracketed notes.
    c) Label the chords using Functional Chord Symbols.
    d) Name the type of Cadence (Authentic or Half).

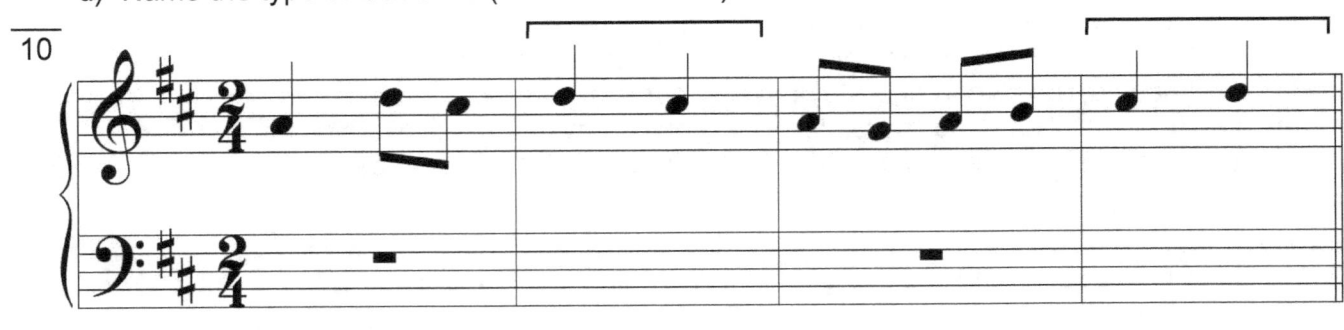

Key: _____   _____ _____   _____ _____

Cadence: _____   Cadence: _____

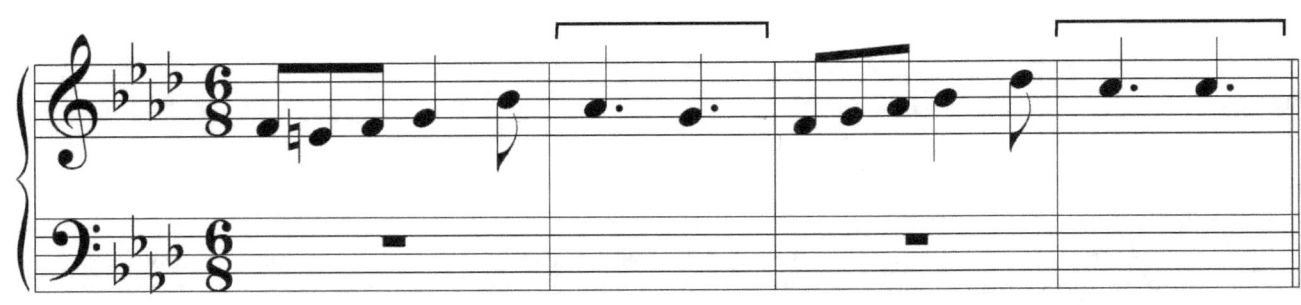

Key: _____   _____ _____   _____ _____

Cadence: _____   Cadence: _____

    d) For each of the following, name the key. Name the type of Cadence (Authentic or Half).

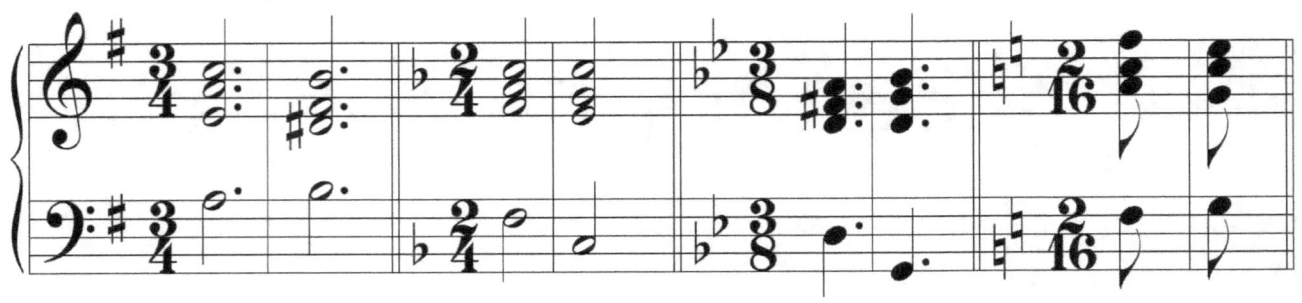

Key: _____   _____   _____   _____

Cadence: _____   _____   _____   _____

7. For the following melody:

    i) Name the key of this melody.

    ii) Compose a four-measure Answer phrase to create a **Contrasting** Period. End on a stable scale degree. (There will be more than one correct answer.)

10   iii) Draw a phrase mark over the Question (Antecedent) phrase and over the contrasting Answer (Consequent) phrase.

    iv) Label the type of cadence (Authentic or Half) at the end of each phrase.

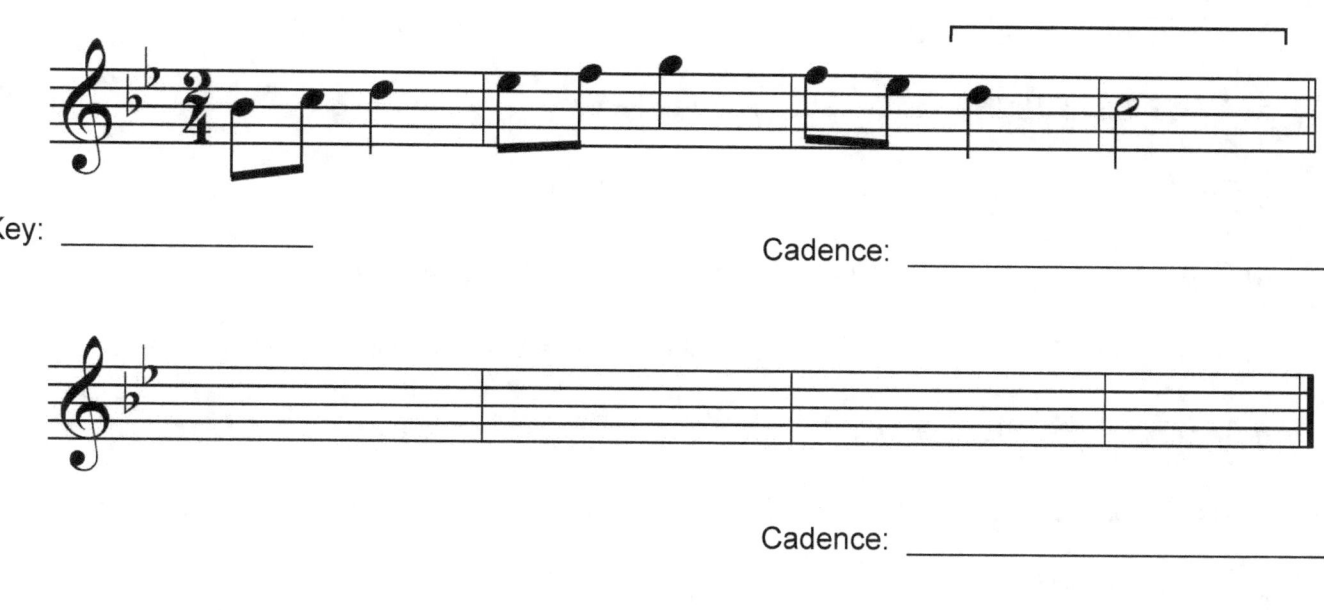

Key: _____

Cadence: _____

Cadence: _____

  b) For the following melody:

    i) Name the key.

    ii) Above the staff, write the Root/Quality Chord Symbol (in root position) outlined by the notes in each measure.

    iii) Below the staff, write the Functional Chord Symbol (in root position) outlined by the notes in each measure.

    iv) Circle and label any passing tones as pt. Circle and label any neighbor tones as nt.

Root/Quality
Chord Symbol: _____   _____   _____   _____

Key: _____

Functional
Chord Symbol: _____   _____   _____   _____

8.   For each of the following terms and signs, circle whether the definition is True or False.

   a) TRUE or FALSE: *sotto voce*   -   return to the original speed

10   b) TRUE or FALSE: *dolente*   -   sad

   c) TRUE or FALSE: *15ma*   -   play one octave higher

   d) TRUE or FALSE: *agitato*   -   moderately slow, at a walking pace

   e) TRUE or FALSE: *tacet*   -   be silent

   f) TRUE or FALSE: *giocoso*   -   humorous, jocose

   g) TRUE or FALSE: *martellato*   -   strongly accented, hammered

   h) TRUE or FALSE: V   -   play the note while drawing the bow downward

   i) TRUE or FALSE: *pesante*   -   expressive, with expression

   j) TRUE or FALSE: 〰   -   continuous slide upward or downward between pitches

   k) TRUE or FALSE: *morendo*   -   dying, fading away

   l) TRUE or FALSE: *grandioso*   -   grand, grandiose

   m) TRUE or FALSE: *semplice*   -   continue in the same manner as has just been played

   n) TRUE or FALSE: *sopra*   -   above

   o) TRUE or FALSE: *vivo*   -   sweet, gentle

   p) TRUE or FALSE: *sostenuto*   -   sustained

   q) TRUE or FALSE: *mesto*   -   marked or stressed

   r) TRUE or FALSE: *risoluto*   -   with some freedom of tempo to enhance expression

   s) TRUE or FALSE: *scherzando*   -   playful, playfully

   t) TRUE or FALSE: *tutti*   -   a passage for the ensemble

9.   Identify the work or the Composer to which each of the following statements applies by placing the appropriate letter in the space provided.

___
10

A - Petrushka
B - Etude in c minor, opus 10, number 12
C - Overture to A Midsummer Night's Dream
D - Dripsody
E - Ko-Ko

F - Felix Mendelssohn
G - Duke Ellington
H - Igor Stravinsky
I - Hugh Le Caine
J - Frédéric Chopin

a) _____ - This Grammy Award Winning American Composer was also a pianist.

b) _____ - This piano piece was nicknamed "Revolutionary".

c) _____ - This Russian Modern Era Composer called himself an "Inventor of Music".

d) _____ - This 20th-Century Canadian Composer was also a Scientist and Physicist.

e) _____ - This jazz piece is in 12-Bar Blues Form and is performed by an orchestra.

f) _____ - This "Poet of the Piano" was born in Poland in the Romantic Era.

g) _____ - This ballet in Rondo Form features polytonality and Pentatonic scales.

h) _____ - This piece of Program Music was inspired by a play by Shakespeare.

i) _____ - This electronic music was created from the recording of a single drop of water.

j) _____ - This German Composer and his sister Fanny wrote music in the Romantic Era.

k) _____ - This Composer played a major role in the development of the Big-Band Era.

l) _____ - This piece features a Polychord - two dissonant chords clashing together.

m) _____ - This piece tells the story of 3 puppets brought to life by a "Magician".

n) _____ - This piece in e flat minor features an Introduction, 7 Choruses and a Coda.

o) _____ - This piece is written in Sonata form (3 distinct sections) in the key of E Major.

p) _____ - This Composer often used "rubato", a free flowing flexible rhythmic tempo.

q) _____ - This Composer created 22 new electronic musical instruments.

r) _____ - This piece is introduced by 4 "Magic Chords" played by Woodwinds and Brass.

s) _____ - This Composer was inducted into the Hollywood Walk of Fame in 1960.

t) _____ - This Composer invented the "Multi-Track", a Special Purpose Tape Recorder.

10. Analyze this excerpt from Swingin' Squirrel by Julianne Warkentin by answering the questions below.

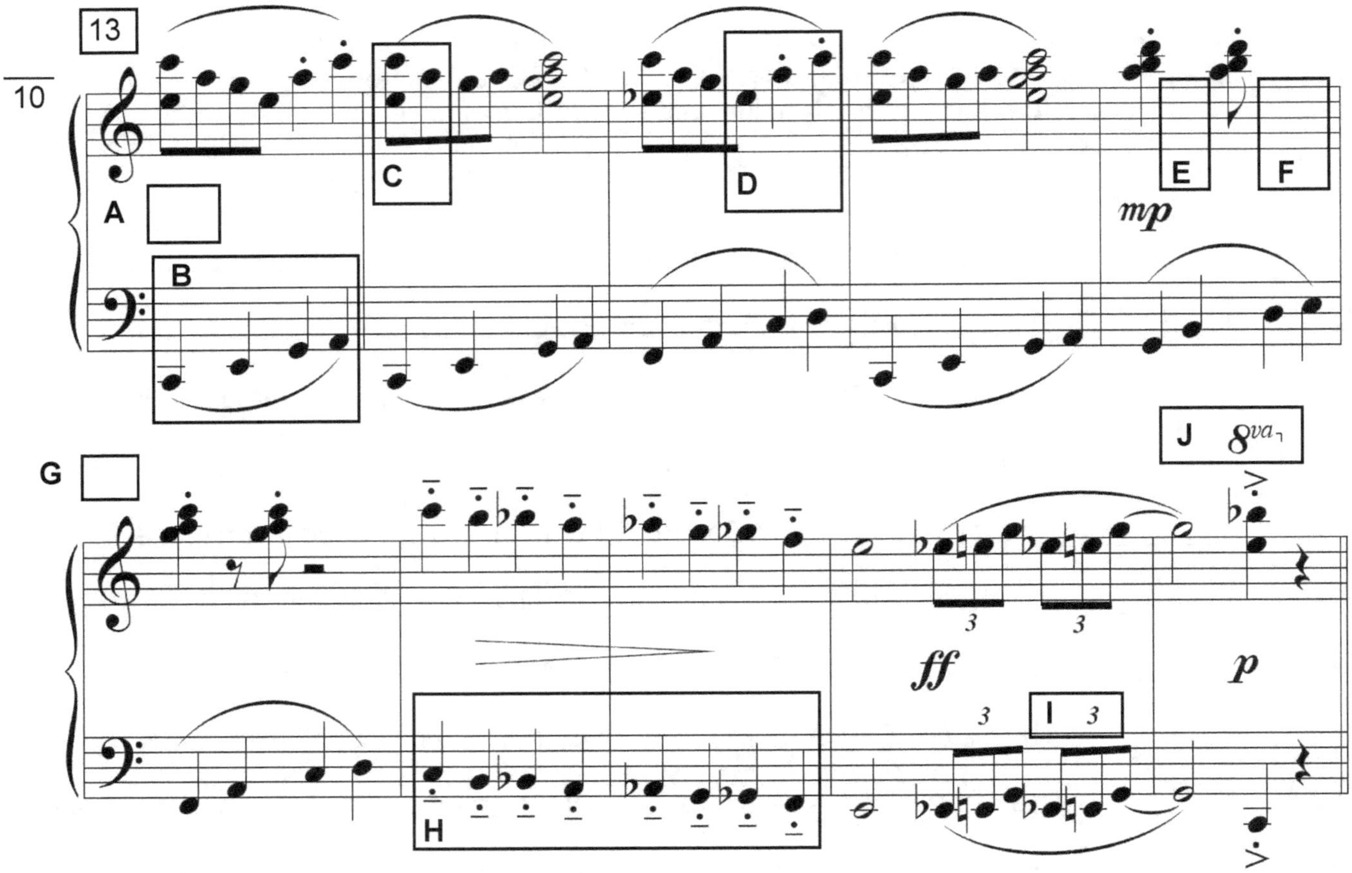

a) At letter **A**, add a dynamic sign to play very loud.

b) Circle a recurrence of the notes (melodic and rhythmic) at letter **B**.

c) For the triad at letter **C**, identify: Root: _____ Quality: _____ Position: _____

d) For the triad at letter **D**, identify: Root: _____ Quality: _____ Position: _____

e) Add the rest at letter **E**. Identify the type of rest used. _____

f) Add the rest at letter **F**. Identify the type of rest used. _____

g) This excerpt begins on Measure 13. Add the missing Measure Number at letter **G**.

h) Identify the type of scale at letter **H**. _____

i) Explain the sign at letter **I**. _____

j) Explain the sign at letter **J**. _____

TOP 10 Ultimate Music Theory Tips
To Score 100% on Exams

Tip #1: Students should complete at least 8 Practice Examinations before writing their Final Exam. LEVEL 7 Exams will have two hours to be completed.

Tip #2: Hold a "Practice Examination" in your studio. Have all students who are writing their Exams come at the same time. They can only bring a ruler, eraser and pencil. Set a Timer. When the timer starts, the examination begins – no talking, no cell phones, no open books!

Tip #3: Pizza Party! On the night before their Examinations, have a "Pizza Party" – Use the Ultimate Music Theory Flashcards App, UMT Whiteboard and UMT Games to review terminology and concepts. Everyone will have fun and everything will be fresh in their minds.

Tip #4: On Exam day, Students should arrive 15 minutes before the start time of their Examination.

Tip #5: If the Student is not given a piece of blank paper to use to write out their UMT Map before beginning their Examination, they should ask for one from the Exam Center Representative. (Have your Student practice asking for a blank piece of paper.)

Tip #6: Remind both Student and Parent that it is the Student's responsibility to bring a mechanical pencil (with extra lead), or 2 - 3 pencils (with a pencil sharpener), eraser and ruler. They cannot bring any items that have "music" on them, so they cannot bring their UMT Rulers.

Tip #7: It is always a good idea to bring a tissue or two, a bottle of water and a couple of hard candies if it is cold/allergy time. Be sure to get plenty of rest the day before the exam.

Tip #8: Complete the exam in order beginning with question 1. Review what your Student can do if they get stuck – if their brain goes blank on a question. One suggestion would be to continue to the next question and then go back later to finish that question.

Tip #9: Remind Students to look at the front AND back of each page to ensure that ALL questions have been answered... and checked... and double checked.

Tip #10: Ultimate Music Theory 100% Club - *The Way to Score Success!* You and your student can become a member of the UMT 100% Club when your student receives a score of 100% on their nationally recognized theory exams including the RCM Theory Examinations.

Go to UltimateMusicTheory.com and complete the UMT 100% Club Form
to receive your special 100% Club Certificate & Congratulations!

ULTIMATE MUSIC THEORY

Workbooks, Exams, Answers, Online Courses, App & More!

A Proven Step-by-Step System to Learn Theory Faster - from Beginner to Advanced.

Innovative techniques designed to develop a complete understanding of music theory, to enhance sight reading, ear training, creativity, composition and musical expression.

All UMT Series have matching Answer Books!

The UMT Rudiments Series - Beginner A, Beginner B, Beginner C, Prep 1, Prep 2, Basic, Intermediate, Advanced & Complete (All-In-One)

♪ 12 Lessons, Review Tests, and a Final Exam to develop confidence
♪ Music Theory Guide & Chart for fast and easy reference of theory concepts
♪ 80 Flashcards for fun drills to dramatically increase retention & comprehension

Rudiments Exam Series - Preparatory, Basic, Intermediate & Advanced

♪ 8 Exams plus UMT Tips on How to Score 100% on Theory Exams

Each Rudiments Workbook correlates to a Supplemental Workbook.

The UMT Supplemental Series - Prep Level, Level 1, Level 2, Level 3, Level 4, Level 5, Level 6, Level 7, Level 8 & Complete (All-In-One) Level

♪ Form & Analysis and Music History - Composers, Eras & Musical Styles
♪ Melody Writing using ICE - Imagine, Compose & Explore
♪ 12 Lessons, Review Tests, Final Exam and 80 Flashcards for quick study

Supplemental Exam Series - Level 5, Level 6, Level 7 & Level 8

♪ 8 Exams to successfully prepare for nationally recognized Theory Exams

UMT Online Courses, Music Theory App & More

♪ UMT Certification Course, Teachers Membership & Elite Educator Program
♪ Ultimate Music Theory App correlates to the Rudiments Workbooks
♪ Free Resources - Teachers Guide, Music Theory Blogs, videos & downloads

Go To: **UltimateMusicTheory.com**